PRACTICING PEACE

PRACTICING PEACE

SPIRITUAL EXERCISES THAT HEAL

W. Glyn Evans

Zondervan Publishing House
Grand Rapids, Michigan

Special acknowledgment to Catherine Jordan for her excellent manuscript
assistance.

Daybreak Books are published by Zondervan Publishing House,
1415 Lake Drive, S.E., Grand Rapids, Michigan 49506.

Library of Congress Cataloging in Publication Data

Evans, W. Glyn (William Glyn)
    Practicing peace.

    1. Spiritual exercises. 2. Spiritual healing. I. Title.
BV4832.2.E86   1987   248.8'6   87-13389
ISBN 0-310-29381-2

Edited by Linda Vanderzalm
Designed by Julie Ackerman Link

Printed in the United States of America

88   89   90   91 / AH / 9   8   7   6   5   4   3   2

To Henrietta, bowstring

CONTENTS

Just as I am, poor, wretched, blind;
Sight, riches, healing of the mind,
  Yea, all I need, in thee to find,
O Lamb of God, I come, I come.
  —Charlotte Elliott

INTRODUCTION

In my years as a pastor, I have learned that many people who claim to be born again are not enjoying total victory in their lives. Just lately, a religious leader sat in my office and said, "I'm having a terrible time relating to my stepmother." This man is a sound Evangelical, an apparently sincere Christian, a church-going person, an outwardly impeccable man, yet he churns with distress over a severely damaged family relationship.

Some time ago I counseled a woman whose life was shattered by drugs and who struggled through the tragic, accidental death of her twenty-year-old daughter. The woman now wavers between believing in God and hating Him for what He has forced her to go through.

It would be easy, logically speaking, to point out the inconsistent attitudes in both the Christian leader and this woman. It would be easy, also, to level a condemning finger at both and say, "Shame on you! Did Jesus Christ die for you, only to see you grovel in defeat and despair over these things?"

I am prevented from doing either because I am aware that

an overwhelming majority of Christians are guilty of the same faults, the same failures, and the same numbing misery as these two friends. The only difference is in the degree to which they experience them.

For years I have wrestled with the question: When Jesus Christ died for us, did He die to heal our emotions also? Obviously *they* were damaged by the Fall as much as our spirits were. Did Jesus die only to reconcile us to God, or did His death also provide reconciliation with ourselves? Is our salvation strictly a spiritual thing or does it include our whole being? Doesn't He also save us from our crippling attitudes like prejudice, resentment, jealousy, envy, and desires to hurt or be hurt?

If our salvation is *whole*, why don't we see evidence of this wholeness? If it is not whole, what hope do we human beings have of becoming more like Christ?

I don't need to remind anyone that negative attitudes can do a job on us. Dr. S. I. McMillen in *None of These Diseases* has shown that negative attitudes can breed an array of physical illnesses. And James Lynch in *The Broken Heart* has documented the effects that loneliness and alienation have on the physical heart.

On the emotional side, Dr. David Seamands shows how those same negative attitudes can cause emotional problems such as anxiety, insecurity, hostility, and the like. His book *Healing for Damaged Emotions* convincingly catalogues the devastating work of negative attitudes that have been allowed to take control of a person's life. In fact, Seamands says, such attitudes can become so entrenched that it becomes almost impossible for a person to believe or trust God or anyone else.

My purpose in writing this book is to add some hope in dealing with poisonous, destructive attitudes. I must honestly say that, as in medicine, the cure will vary from person to person.

Introduction

The same medicine that will cure one person will cause a flurry of side effects for another person.

So what I say in this book may not help everyone. But I have every confidence that in the hands of God it will touch enough people and bring them sufficient relief to justify its writing.

How have I gone about it?

Basically, I have built a ground work of *hope* throughout. I insist that God has a solution for every problem and that it is possible to build a relationship with Him in which His healing power permeates our entire beings. I believe very strongly that hope, properly grounded and sincerely accepted, not only can become the beginning of dramatic changes in attitude but also will result in healing.

When I think of hope, I think of Dr. Bernard Siegel, a teacher of surgery at Yale University School of Medicine. According to journalist Michael J. McManus, Siegel is a firm believer in hope as an effective healer in both the physical and emotional areas of suffering. Dr. Siegel says: "I teach people how to hope and to pray—tools that are outside the realm of medicine." Early in his practice he discovered that people who "made it," people who got well, were "survivors." They were the people who said, "I loved. I forgave. I accepted. I had faith. I hoped. And I made it." And Dr. Siegel has seen miracles happen as a result of that attitude.

What Dr. Siegel discovered is not new, but the *practice* of it is. We all know that negative, defeatist attitudes can destroy us, while positive, upbeat attitudes bring us serenity and victory.

With this fact in mind, I have based this book on the healing power of the gospel as we adopt its principles in our daily lives. I have done this by assuming that the gospel of Jesus Christ is sufficient for all the needs of the whole person. The gospel not only heals "spiritually" but heals wrong attitudes, wrong impulses, wrong character traits, and wrong impressions.

13

Practicing Peace

Yes, I have seen the gospel change not only people's wrong *behavior* but also their wrong *orientation*.

What I have tried to do in this book is to show how we can escape from our negative thinking and therefore become positive. I have done this by showing how the ordinary practices of the Christian life—praising, confessing, loving, forgiving, believing, hoping, praying, reading the Bible, and sharing with others—are all natural gospel components that enable us to be spiritually and emotionally victorious.

The second major emphasis in this book is *appropriation*. The word *appropriate* is defined by *Webster's Dictionary* as "to take exclusive possession of." This book urges believers to take exclusive possession of the healing properties of the gospel of Jesus Christ.

But that's the difficulty!

In my pastoral experience, I have worked with many hundreds of people in all aspects of their Christian lives, and I say without the slightest hesitation that the greatest barrier to their (and my) living healed and victorious lives is *the failure to appropriate what is ours.*

Now let me be more specific. The failure to appropriate is caused by two kinds of attitudes: The "I can'ts" and the "I won'ts."

I must admit that a small minority of believers just can't appropriate God's available help. People who are biologically deprived—those who suffered brain damage at birth, those who are genetically unable to function at normal levels, and those who suffer from various kinds of diseases—find it extremely difficult to practice appropriation.

Dr. John White, whose masterful *The Masks of Melancholy* has pioneered new trails for the Christian therapist, comments: "Some patients who have been receiving counseling for years have been made well in a couple of months once the

14

real problem (depression caused by chemical imbalance) has been sorted out" (p. 77). In other words, when a chemical imbalance creates the depression, no amount of appropriation will produce a cure, unless God performs a miracle. The cause is physical. These kinds of people, says White, may be counseled to seek God's forgiveness, to distrust their feelings, or to obey—but they cannot. Therefore they begin to think they are not Christians at all. The problem is "they can't," not "they won't."

Now let's turn to the "I won'ts." This is where most of us live. And there may be many reasons for it (though perhaps not *justified* reasons).

Consider the "druther be mad" attitude. This was the response of the boy who had fought with his brother. The boy was sent out into the yard to cool off and think matters over. When his father went out after a lapse of time to ask if he wanted to come back into the house, the boy replied, "Nope, druther be mad!"

Some of us *like* to be negative. It's a kind of compensation, like revenge. We didn't get what we wanted, so we make everybody around us pay for it by making them suffer our hostility or alienation.

Or look at the *familiarity* aspect. Maybe we don't want to be saints (in practice) because we are quite comfortable with the way we are, faults and all. It's like the prisoner in the Paris Bastille who, when he was offered liberation on the day the Bastille fell in 1789, said to his liberators: "No, I don't want to leave. This is home to me."

Another reason could be the "what's wrong with *me?*" attitude. This is the attitude of the Christian who says, "Sure, I've got faults. Hasn't everybody?" The sweeping inclusion makes the person feel smug and secure. The person justifies a miserable future by convincing himself or herself that this is normal life.

I was reminded of this when I thought of Job's astonishing admission to God. "'My ears had heard of you but now my eyes have seen you'" (Job 42:5). In other words, "I thought I knew you, but I really didn't until just now." The result of that clear flash of insight made Job not only see God but also see *himself.* So he went on, "'Therefore, I despise myself and repent in dust and ashes'" (Job 42:6).

Most of the "I won'ts" have never had a clear look at God or themselves, otherwise they would groan in despair. But that groan of despair would quickly lead them to change their "I won't" to an "I will," and appropriation would begin immediately.

I don't mean to imply that appropriating is always an easy thing to do. Take the example of the parents whose soldier son is terror-bombed while serving his country overseas. Or the young woman who is dragged from a parking lot and raped.

It's not easy to bounce back from these life-sapping experiences and start appropriating. Trust, confidence, and faith have been brutally shattered, and they must be nursed back to wholeness again. That's why appropriating is always a *patient* work. So let's be patient with the Lord, ourselves, and each other.

In every part of this book I have tried to nudge us all toward a posture of appropriation because there, I believe, is where the secret of wholeness and victory lies. Now the rest is up to each of us. Jesus once said to His disciples, "'Come and have breakfast'" (John 21:12). He had made full provision for them and had proffered the invitation. But He couldn't eat for them. That's where appropriation came in.

Let's respond to our Lord's gracious invitation. Let's come and have a meal with Him!

1

THE HEALING POWER OF
PRAISE

A pastor in California, a perfectionist with a tremendous amount of drive and ambition, developed migraine headaches. Whenever they occurred, he was so devastated by the pain and misery that he had to go to bed. One night when he was scheduled to lead a meeting in his home, he was so overwhelmed by a headache that he could hardly move his body, much less climb out of bed. He wondered how he could get up and lead that meeting.

Then he seemed to hear a voice deep inside him. It said, "Praise Me." He recognized the voice as the Lord's. He recognized also that this command was a challenge to his faith. God was saying in effect, "Praise Me and see what wonders I will do." Perplexed by the Lord's strange request, he dragged himself from his bed and entered the living room. Then he began the meeting with the loudest hymn of praise he could find in the book. As the meeting progressed, his headache diminished, then left him completely. He finished the meeting with vibrant joy.

The pastor learned something valuable that night—that praise ("faith singing") is a powerful expression of faith that results in a displacement of pain by the power of God.

Praise is a melodious expression of our faith in God's person, His word, and His power. Praise frees us from bondage and releases God's power within us so that God is able to work out everything for our good. Praise forcibly drives out doubt, suspicion, jealousy, bitterness, anxiety, depression, and other dark moods that often result from our difficulties and that hinder the coming of joy in our lives. In short, praise relaxes us. We cannot fume and fret and praise at the same time.

Praise is not just a state of mind, as Dr. Emile Coué, the French psychotherapist, would have us believe. Dr. Coué felt that if a sick person acted well ("Everyday, in every way, I am getting better"), that person would be well. Basically, this is a denial of pain. But praise doesn't deny pain; it displaces it. It displaces it by exercising faith in God's healing and restoring power.

To praise honestly and sincerely is to believe. Just as you cannot pray sincerely and hate at the same time, you cannot praise God and doubt Him at the same time. It is faith that gives God the opportunity to send His healing power flooding through us.

All negative feelings are displaced by a sincere, whole-hearted expression of praise to God, whether in word, music, or thought. Feelings of bitterness, malice, clamor, envy, intolerance, revenge, hatred, jealousy, and any other mind-destroying attitudes can be displaced by praise. Everyone knows that two solid bodies cannot inhabit the same space. Likewise the spiritual person knows that praise and negative feelings cannot cohabit the same mind.

Medical doctors have learned this. Dr. Walter L. Wilson of Kansas City, Missouri, was a practicing physician before he gave up medicine to preach the gospel. Once he was treating a woman whose attitude toward life had turned sour. Everyone was against her, nothing was going right, life was unfair, and God was no longer her friend. After determining that nothing was physically wrong with her, Dr. Wilson said, "I've got a prescription here that I want you to take three times a day. Don't miss one dose."

"What is it?" she asked suspiciously.

"I want you to sing all the verses of 'Count Your Many Blessings.'"

Too astonished to reply, the woman left his office and later, intrigued by the novelty of the advice, she began to do as he had ordered. In a few days her symptoms left her.

No one needs to be told that Psalm 23 exudes a cheerful confidence in our Great Shepherd. Many Christians have told me that when they cannot sleep at night, the recitation of this beautiful praise poem is all they need to relax and fall asleep.

A friend of mine who was a patient of the renowned Chicago psychiatrist, Dr. William S. Sadler, once told me that Sadler strongly believed in the Bible as a potent instrument in healing diseased minds. He told her, "To read the Bible and believe it, especially such portions as Psalm 23, is far better medicine than anything I can give you."

Perhaps this is why God is so emphatic in commanding us to praise. Paul is unequivocal in this. "Give thanks in all circumstances, for this is God's will for you in Christ Jesus" (1 Thess. 5:18). Paul sees praise not merely as an item of worship reserved for Sunday morning services but as a heart-

and-mind attitude that spells victory over the nagging, worri-some problems of life. When I praise God for everything, I am simply committing my faith to action, risking everything for His sake. God is honored by that kind of leap toward Him. And the praiser is helped.

The Bible equates praise with God Himself. "He is your praise" (Deut. 10:21). This means more than God is the *source* or *object* of our praise. God's praise and glory are directly related. To praise God is to ascribe the highest honor to His name, as expressed in the Psalm: "Whoso offereth praise glorifieth me" (Ps. 50:23 KJV). We can glorify God in many ways, but praising Him stands at the top. To praise God means to assent to His person, to accept His will, and to agree joyously with all His plans and purposes.

That's why the opposite of praise—murmuring, grum-bling, complaining, whining—are viewed as indirect insults to God's person and ways. It was this sin that caused God to leave the bones of the wandering Israelites to whiten in the Sinai desert (Ps. 95:8–11). Criticism had displaced praise in their mouths, and without praise the Israelites could not give God His rightful honor and glory. Paul warns us to avoid their sad example: "And do not grumble, as some of them did—and were killed by the destroying angel" (1 Cor. 10:10).

The Book of Psalms is the unique praise book of the Bible. The King James Version uses the word "praise" no less than 153 times in its various grammatical expressions. Praise is an attractive compliment to God. "Sing joyfully to the LORD, you righteous; it is fitting for the upright to praise him" (Ps. 33:1). The word "fitting" ("comely" KJV) means "becoming," "suitable," or "beautiful." We are always beautiful to God, despite our sins, but never so much as when we praise Him.

20

The Healing Power of Praise

THE BIBLICAL FOUNDATIONS OF PRAISE

Praise demonstrates a firm confidence in God's ability, control, and power. In order to arrive at this point, I must come to grips with that amazing absolute: "And we know that in all things God works for the good of those who love him, who have been called according to his purpose" (Rom. 8:28).

Every Christian must grapple with the absolute contained in this verse. It is summed up in the two words: "all things." Many Christians have difficulties with this at one time or another. To them "all things" become "some things" or "few things." Or perhaps doubt may lead them to another rendering: "Maybe all things do; I can't be sure."

I agree that it's difficult for a Christian going through a divorce to accept this absolute. And what about the girl who has been raped or the young mother who has been told she has incurable cancer?

At this point Christians have a choice: We can either accept the absolute in this verse or deny it. If we accept it, it means we are confident and assured about God's intent to bring beauty out of ashes, something glorious out of something horrible. Once we reach that confidence the next obvious step is praise.

Praise, therefore, is a joyous affirmation of God's determination to overcome all evil in my life and make it yield good. Praise is grounded in God's power.

Notice how Jesus felt about disappointment and frustration. See how he demonstrated praiseful living. Things went well for Him during His first year of public ministry—great crowds, many miracles, much enthusiasm. Then the people of Capernaum, Bethsaida, and Chorazin turned against Him and His message. Christ's reaction was the "Woe" speech recorded in Matthew 11:20–24. Yet, despite His keen disappointment with the people of those cities, Jesus "rejoiced in spirit" and thanked His heavenly Father that God's will was being done, "for so it seemed good in thy sight" (Matt. 11:26; Luke 10:21 KJV).

Jesus responded to a crushing upset by rejoicing in His spirit. Although He must have rejoiced continually, this is the only Gospel record of Jesus "rejoicing." And it came after one of His biggest disappointments.

Why did Jesus take this disappointment jubilantly? Because He knew the Father was working everything out for good in the life of His Son. Because Jesus believed this bedrock fact, He lived praisefully. He offered to His Father a continual sacrifice of praise.

Praise shows firm confidence in God's love. The Bible says God loves me (John 3:16). It also says He loves me everlastingly (Jer. 31:3). It even says He loves me regardless of my spiritual condition (Rom. 5:8). Now if I can accept as fact this second absolute—God's faithful, never-ending, unwavering love—this fact will lead me to the proper response of praise.

Praise understands what God's love is. God's way of looking at us and feeling about us makes it impossible for Him to hurt us willingly or permanently. Despite His rigorous discipline, which is designed to make us more comformable to His will, God's love speaks of His determination to treat us as supremely valuable. He is after our good, nothing less. And His great power accomplishes what His love desires for us.

If I can grasp this fact today and make it one of the foundations of my thinking, I would do nothing but praise Him. What other love can match His? What other being could have so much self-sacrificing interest in us? What other helper can exert so much effort on our behalf simply because he or she loves us? No one in earth or heaven, however dear that person may be!

The Healing Power of Praise

Praise, therefore, is the joyous affirmation that God loves me with a quality of love found nowhere else—all for my benefit. His love will never disappear, turn cold, or turn to hate.

Praise shows firm confidence in God's partnership with us, as expressed in Paul's words: "If God is for us, who can be against us?" (Rom. 8:31). This verse, if I understand it correctly, means that God takes the part of His children against all enemies.

By accepting me because of Jesus Christ, God is committed to working for me and in me. That means He leads me according to His will in spite of difficulties, opposition, satanic harassment, fears, doubts, or whatever. With God on my side, I have almightiness on my side. I must always remember that evil is not almighty, God is.

No matter what obstacle may confront me, God's almightiness is pitted against it. No problem, difficulty, or impossibility can terrorize or paralyze Him. Thus I have the key to unlimited power to help me with my problem. That's why I can afford to sing praises in the face of my difficulties. Praise says I recognize God's almightiness, and that almightiness is in full support of *me*.

Praise is never merely a *feeling*, although one of the chief results of praise is joy. Rather praise is an act of the will based on facts. If my praise to God is based on my emotions rather than my will, my praise won't last long.

When I praise God, I have already come to a decision deep down in my heart: I will stake my all on Him. I claim His love for me. I submit to His power to make all things work for my good. I stand on His promise to back me to the hilt against everything that threatens me.

Praise is the result, not the cause, of this decision. It is because these facts are true that I am able to raise my voice and sing. And when I sing, my mind clears out all negative, destructive feelings and fills me with the joy of the Lord instead.

PRAISE HEALS

I have often experienced a healing of the mind by simply praising God. One day, full of mind-tearing frustration, I went for a walk. A good Christian friend and I had had a sharp disagreement over policy matters in our fellowship. At the same time the bank in which my older son worked had come perilously close to declaring bankruptcy. His job and future were clouded with uncertainty. Also at the same time, my daughter was struggling to overcome the effects of a bitter and painful experience.

As I walked, I could feel the mental agony of not being able to put it all together. Nothing made sense. Romans 8:28 seemed to be a hollow mockery. I felt like lashing out at God for what seemed to be His callous, studied indifference to my problems.

But then the "still, small voice" of the Spirit spoke to me as I trudged on. The message seemed to be, "Think of all the good things I've done for you and praise Me for them."

That quieted me. I began to reflect on all the things God had given to me or had done for me during my several decades of serving Him. I remembered the beginning when God seemed to come out of nowhere and stood astride my path. There I met Him, yielded my will to Him, and came to know His love in the most personal and real way. Throughout the years He added blessing on blessing: wife, children, fruit in ministry, friends, supply of needs, many answers to prayer. It would be tedious to mention them all. But I was awed and humbled at both the quantity and quality of blessing He had lavished on me.

Then came the humbling that Job experienced. Spiritually I sat in ashes and repented of my sin of forgetfulness and ingratitude. Repeatedly I lifted my voice inwardly to praise Him for all He had done. Tears flowed and feelings were released. Gradually I could sense the displacement of my hostility and frustration with peace and joy. By the end of my two-and-a-half-mile walk I was conscious of having been thoroughly purged and renewed. And for *that* I added an extra "Praise the Lord!" Yes, praise releases us from the bondage of our destructive, dark feelings.

Dr. William P. Wilson discovered the healing power of spiritual principles in practicing psychiatry. One patient had been in and out of his office for two years with one of the worst cases of bitterness he had ever seen. This woman simply seethed with anger against her husband, and the anger had stretched over an unbelievable twenty years!

Nothing the doctor did seemed to help. As a last resort he asked the woman about her religious faith. She was a church member, she said, but the church met none of her needs. Pressing the matter, Wilson told her she needed a personal relationship with Jesus Christ.

She asked, "How do I get this personal relationship?"

The doctor then explained how she could become a Christian, and he documented his presentation with Scripture passages.

When he finished, she asked querulously, "Why hasn't anyone told me about Him before?"

The woman received Christ, and in time her bitterness disappeared. She not only received the power to forgive, but she also received the strength to praise God for all things and to live a life of humble gratitude. (*Christian Reader*, January/February 1975, p. 64.)

I, too, know the destructive power of anger and resentment. I can testify to the misery they have wrought in my life. I can also remember the patient, persistent instruction of the Lord: "Accept what I send you joyously. Don't fight my interventions. I mean them for your good. Don't worry if your pride is hurt.

Praise me for all I am doing to you, and my joy will continue to be your strength. See my hand and purpose in everything." Once I learned this lesson and practiced it, I saw Him banish the gloomy mist of defeat and misery. I have learned that joyful acceptance of His dealings with me invariably brings me into the sunshine.

I must always try to live the gentle life, the life of acceptance that enables God to inhabit my praises (Ps. 22:3 KJV). Basically, the life of praise begins and ends with God. It is because of who He is and who I am that my praising results in His being properly honored and my being properly blessed. When I reach this stage, I have learned what Jeremiah Burroughs called "the rare jewel of Christian contentment."

The cultivation of a thankful spirit is not confined to Christians. Unsaved people know the psychological benefit of such an attitude, also. Non-Christian, emotionally mature people often adopt the outlook that no matter what happens in life, something positive can be learned. This confidence and assurance is what William James, early twentieth-century psychologist, called the "enthusiasm of self-surrender." This is not the "spiritual" self-surrender of the New Testament sense but the psychological self-surrender that enables the person to deal positively and hopefully with every adverse part of life's drama. The result, says James, is that the person "becomes unified and consciously right, superior and happy."

If non-believers can move their psychological resources toward this kind of serene, joyous living, what about believers in Jesus Christ? With more than our own resources available to us, can't we do as much or even more to bring ourselves to the place of triumphant soaring? Of course! We are promised life more abundantly (John 10:10). We are assured that everything that happens to us will work out for our good (Rom. 8:28). We are guaranteed the presence of God at all times (Heb. 13:5). We are given a Helper—the Paraclete, the Holy Spirit—whose responsibility is to see that we arrive home safely (John 14:16–17). We are provided with "a spirit of power, of love and of self-discipline" (2 Tim. 1:7) to assure that we will not be overcome by any spirit of timidity or fear.

So the Christians' family relationship to God furnishes them with every boost and enables them to mount to the level of praiseful and joyful living.

But how do we do it? How do we banish the gloom and darkness and cultivate the spirit of grateful praise? How do we do it when we don't *feel* like doing it?

The key is the will. The issue is "feeling versus willing." If we consult our feelings, we will never become overcoming persons. We must *will* it. It takes a great deal of energy to will what we don't feel, but once we determine to follow through, the law of the Spirit and the mind will begin to operate.

We must always remember that the will is the key. From then on it is a matter of practice. You may want to begin by practicing this "Declaration of Praise":

Lord,

• I take my stand that everything in my life is working together for my good. I praise You for it.

• I believe with all my heart that You love me with an everlasting love, and nothing can change it. I praise You for it.

• I am firmly convinced that with You on my side, nothing can stand against me, and therefore I have Your mighty resources to help me in this need. For this I praise You.

• I am convinced that praising You is one of my highest acts of worship. Therefore I praise You as the proper, creaturely thing to do.

- I believe that praise is an affirmation of my faith in You and therefore releases the power of the Holy Spirit to work mightily in me. For this I praise You.

- I am persuaded that praise is the very opposite of complaining and grumbling and that it banishes the spirit of murmuring in me. I praise You, Lord.

- I am convinced that resentment, hatred, bitterness, and all their ills are offensive to you. Therefore, I will banish them with an expression of praise to You and thus put You back on the throne of my heart.

- I will praise You for Yourself, Your Son, Your Spirit, Your Word, Your creation, and all the gifts of loved ones and provisions You have wonderfully given me.

- I will praise You because You are the ultimate Victor over all evil, and I will begin that victory in my heart through praise.

- I will praise you every day and every way, in good times or bad, that Your praise may lighten my life and radiate to others for Your own name's sake.

Amen.

A good friend of mine, a sincere Christian, was dying of cancer. The day before he died, God revealed to him that he would soon be called home to heaven. He also instructed him to leave a message to be shared with his family, fellow Christians, and friends. The message was very simple: "Tell them to keep praising Me." To all who came to see my friend in the final hours, the message was the same: "Keep praising God." On the brink of eternity, this man spoke an eternal word. There can be no greater advice to impart to people—especially God's people.

The Healing Power of Praise

This message is well worth heeding, for the Lord's sake and also for our own.

I have adversity in my life. Everyone does. I face difficulty all the time, not just periodically. To try to be free of adversity is a hopeless quest. It is self-defeating and destroying. The secret is to overcome adversity not by eliminating it (which can't happen) nor by denying it (which is self-deception) but by conquering it with praise.

Praise versus adversity is no contest. Praise wins every time. Praise says, "I know you are there, adversity, but I will render you powerless to hurt me by praising God for you. I know He is working out His will through you. I believe you are a friend, not a foe. I believe that God will handle you in a way most conducive to my prosperity and blessing. I am convinced that you have no power to harm me because your power has been given to you from above. I cannot fight you, or I will lose my health and sanity. I cannot ignore you, or I would be blind or insane. But I can praise you into submission because I call on a higher power to handle you and make you work out my ultimate good. Adversity, I salute you! You are a servant of God to me. Your mask is ugly and horrible, but behind it is the face of ultimate kindness and beneficent love. Adversity, you must bow and submit before the 'all things' of Romans 8:28. And for that I exult in God my Savior."

2

THE HEALING POWER OF
CONFESSION

On the wall of his home in Boulder, Colorado, a friend of mine has hung this motto:

> Nothing worse can be said of me than what God already said—
> I am a sinner.
> And nothing better can be said of me than what God has already said—
> I am His child.

The most deplorable condition of the human race is sin. The most blessed is the forgiveness that God offers in Jesus

Christ. That's what this chapter is all about: how sin enslaves us and how confession heals and restores us. By confession I mean admitting that we have sinned or done wrong. The prodigal son said, "I will set out and go back to my father and say to him: 'Father, I have sinned against heaven and against you'" (Luke 15:18). That's confession.

SIN ENSLAVES US

Sin devastates us spiritually. Sin alienates us, shuts us out from God's presence, and leaves us to muddle through on our own. Before we can begin to be restored, we must get back in tune with God. And it's possible. How grateful we ought to be for God's grace that forgives us and restores us to His fellowship and favor once again. This forgiveness was made legally possible through the work of Jesus on the cross. It is made practically possible when we become aware of our sinfulness and take the initiative to ask God for cleansing and restoration.

Sin devastates us physically. Too little attention is paid to the physical effects of human sin, despite the clear statements in Genesis telling us that as a result of Adam's sin, we will "labor" and "sweat" and "toil painfully" all the days of our lives. In other words, the human body is to suffer from physical stress because of sin (Gen. 3:17–19).

The vast evidence of human experience only confirms what the Bible says. Dr. S. I. McMillen has catalogued ten classes of bodily disorders that are affected by stressful living: disorders of the digestive system, circulatory system, genito-urinary system, nervous system, and glandular system; disorders of the eyes and skin; disorders of the muscle-joint units; disorders of the allergic defenses; as well as disorders of the immune system. Of course McMillen does not claim that these disorders are caused by stress alone, but they *can* be. And if they are not *caused* by stress, then certainly they are *aggravated* by it.

The Healing Power of Confession

The Bible gives us a graphic account of acute physical stress brought about by sin in the story of David's sin of adultery with Bathsheba (2 Sam. 11). While his army was besieging Rabbah in Moab, David stayed behind in Jerusalem. One night from his rooftop he saw a beautiful woman, Bathsheba, bathing. Smitten by her beauty, he sent for her and committed adultery with her. Later in trying to cover up his sin (which was "discovered" because Bathsheba became pregnant), David ordered Bathsheba's husband, Uriah the Hittite, to be killed in the front line of the battle at Rabbah (2 Sam. 11:14). Thus to adultery David added the gruesome sin of murder.

Psalm 32 describes the acute pain David felt in his soul, conscience, and body while he "kept silent" (did not confess his sin). "My bones wasted away," David complained. He was not old, yet his body felt old because of his sin. As a result he kept groaning all day long. David cried out that God's hand was heavy upon him, causing his conscience to sting and pain. He could not be legally prosecuted for killing Uriah—he had neatly arranged all that. But he couldn't escape the outrage of his conscience. The psalmist recalls that his strength was sapped as in the heat of summer, possibly referring to recurrent fever because of his emotional upset.

"Unforgiven sin," says Dr. Paul Tournier, the Swiss psychologist, "is a clog on human vitality." Because of the incredibly close interaction between mind and body, the human body can become one of the casualties of sin. Jesus implied as much when He said to the paralyzed man whom He had healed: "See, you are well again. Stop sinning or something worse may happen to you" (John 5:14).

Dr. Hans Selye, former director of the University of Montreal's Institute of Experimental Medicine and Surgery, experimented for ten years to discover why the human body, wonderfully resistant to disease as it is, succumbs to degenerative diseases like high blood pressure, arthritis, arteriosclerosis, and heart trouble. His conclusion: unrelenting stress and tension is often a cause and is always a contributing factor in these diseases.

Sin (especially unconfessed sin) is one of the many causes of unrelenting stress in human beings. Therefore sin in any of its forms exacts a fearful toll from our bodies.

The range of sin is wide and troublesome. Overt sins like stealing, adultery, lying, and so forth will certainly arouse the conscience, especially if the person (such as a Christian) is taught to avoid them. The finer the sensitization, the greater the pain if that sensitivity is bruised.

Once I was invited to have dinner with a midwestern family in whose church I had been preaching. The husband, Tom (not his real name), seemed shaky and tense both during the meal and afterward. It made me wonder about him. Later in the day I mentioned his uneasiness to one of the elders and he said, "Ask Tom about it. He'll be glad to tell you."

The next week I did. Tom seemed relieved when I brought up the matter. "I wanted to tell you last week," he said, "but I didn't have the nerve."

"What is it?" I asked.

"I have stolen company funds," he replied, "and since it is a criminal offense, I am to appear in court in a few weeks. I'm sweating that out."

Tom then gave me a detailed description of his thievery. He squandered the money on household gadgets—a new television set, a new stereo set, and other material signs of wealth. He explained his increased flow of funds to his wife as a series of "bonuses" from the company. His wife at first rejoiced at their new-found prosperity.

Then Tom's conscience began to stir, affecting his body, which began to suffer. His pulse rate increased as did his blood pressure. His appetite waned, and he began to lose weight. Nighttime brought no relief, and dawn often found him still tossing and turning. His wife grew worried.

Finally Tom confessed to her what he had done. Horror-struck, she listened to his astounding disclosure. Later they sought refuge in prayer and begged God to forgive Tom's crime. They continued until they found assurance that God had granted forgiveness.

Next they decided Tom should confess to the company and offer to make restitution. His employers were saddened but had no alternative except to discharge Tom and turn the matter over to the district attorney.

That's when I had dinner with the family. Tom obviously was feeling better since he made a clean breast of everything and was hopeful of a favorable court decision. But he will never forget the suffering he brought on himself and his family.

In all this Tom had one advantage. His sin was *overt*, which meant that sooner or later it would eventuate in a crisis and then everything would be out in the open.

Not so with covert sins. Anger, resentment, bitterness, jealousy, and so forth are not crimes; they are sins of the spirit. They can linger undetected for years, and yet all the while they punish the body severely. Too often they are explained away as personality quirks, "That's the way he (she) is." A well-known professor of medicine in Europe used to instruct his students: "Confess your patient." By this he meant: Get your patient to confess his faults, his sense of failure, his feelings of bitterness and anger. He had learned through many years of experience that a disturbed spirit can create or facilitate many bodily ills and that confession often removes the hindrances to healing.

Scientists are now achieving breakthroughs in the under-standing of how stress affects the body's immune system. They have discovered that stress of a sufficient quantity and duration will release in the brain, chemical opiate-like substances that will render the immune system less able to deal with such things as killer viruses, the growth of cancer cells, and so forth. Other studies have shown that stress overly stimulates the pituitary gland, which affects the adrenal glands, which in turn can affect almost every organ of the body.

I saw the effect of prolonged stress on Robert DeVane. Robert seemed to be a physical weakling, thin and lacking vigor and vitality. He was chronically depressed. He was under constant medical care, although the doctors never diagnosed him as really ill.

His mother was a large, self-assured woman with a keen mind and a deep love for God and His Word. Because she felt Robert, her only son, was naturally weak, she showered him with care all the way to adulthood.

One day Robert came to see me. He explained how miserable he felt most of the time. He had little or no appetite, was chronically tired, and was deeply resentful of his mother.

"Your mother?" I asked in surprise.

"Yes, my mother. She always treats me like a baby. She won't let me live my own life. I want to get married, but that idea makes her furious. She says it would be a disaster. I get angry at her, but my conscience bothers me. Then I have to confess my sin. But the problem won't go away."

"Are you *sure* it's your mother, Robert?" I raised the question, still unconvinced.

"I'm positive!"

When he left, he was still miserable and I was still doubtful.

The answer came some months later when his mother suddenly and unexpectedly died. As I busied myself with the funeral, I asked myself repeatedly, "What's going to happen to Robert?"

The Healing Power of Confession

Robert himself provided the answer. Within a year he married a fine young woman who belonged to the church that he attended. He grew physically stronger and more robust. His energy level rose. He became less depressed and confused and began to take an active part in church matters. Later he was elected to be a deacon. He and his wife developed a beautiful husband-wife relationship, and their home became a haven of hospitality that was a model to the whole congregation.

Now of course I can see that Robert's problem had been a deep resentment of his mother's overbearing attitude toward him. This resentment created a stress that resulted in the malfunctioning of his body. He was unable to overcome that resentment until the problem "went away."

Sin also affects us psychologically. There is no doubt that unconfessed and undealt with sin affects the mind just as directly as it affects the body, perhaps more so. Swiss psychotherapist Carl Jung said, "Nature will punish the man who will not come clean."

Psychological stress due to sin began simultaneously with the birth of sin. Adam and Eve suffered not only the *physical* consequences of their disobedience but also the *emotional* results. Adam and Eve experienced an awakening consciousness that they never felt before: "The eyes of them both were opened, and they knew . . ." (Gen. 3:7 KJV). Their eyes were "opened," indicating the dawning consciousness of guilt. Quickly following in the wake of guilt came shame and fear. So in a very short time, perhaps hours at the most, three feelings found birth in the souls of our first parents. The pattern is exactly the same today when we disobey God's standards.

The classic biblical example of an injured conscience is that of Saul, the first king of Israel. Although Saul began his reign with a humble attitude and gratifying success, he began to grow proud and arrogant. The peak of his self-sufficiency occurred when God told him to wipe out the Amalekites (1 Sam. 15). God had told him to destroy everything totally. But Saul hedged on the "everything" and instead spared the best sheep and cattle. This was a flagrant violation of God's order and a selfish taking of the spoil for his own use.

God's response to Saul's high-handed disobedience was rejection: "Because you have rejected the word of the LORD, he has rejected you as king" (1 Sam. 15:23). This rejection was a devastating blow to Saul. In desperation he went through the charade of confessing his sin, begging for "honor" before the elders. In other words his confession was not contrition before God but merely an empty form that he hoped would pacify God on the one hand yet not allow him to lose face with the elders on the other.

The pretense did not work. God withdrew from Saul and sent Samuel to find another king. That's when depression struck Saul for the first time. The Spirit of the Lord left Saul, and an evil or harmful spirit tormented him.

Alarmed at their king's tormented mental state, Saul's advisers sought a harp player to soothe him. David was found and the result was, at first, a beneficial one. "Whenever the spirit from God came upon Saul, David would take his harp and play. Then relief would come to Saul; he would feel better, and the evil spirit would leave him" (1 Sam. 16:23).

However, this musical therapy was quickly disrupted when Saul became jealous of David's military exploits, especially David's victory over the Philistine giant Goliath. The adulation of the crowds expressed in the chant, "Saul has slain his thousands, and David his tens of thousands" goaded the king to insane jealousy. His depression grew worse as the "Spirit from God came *forcefully* upon Saul" (1 Sam. 18:10, emphasis added). The pressure eventually twisted his reason, and Saul tried to kill David with a javelin. From then on David became a hunted man fleeing from Saul's rage.

The Healing Power of Confession

The connecting links of Saul's downfall are easily seen. First, he disobeyed the orders of the Lord because he wanted to enrich himself. Second, he refused to repent sincerely of his sin. Third, he resented David's rise to power and popularity. And fourth, he tried to murder the newly anointed successor to his throne.

Saul could have avoided the bitter results of rebellion by a sincere and honest humbling of himself before God in confession. Would God have forgiven him? Did the same God not forgive David later for *his* sin (Ps. 51)?

Saul's history illustrates the psychological damage that we bring on ourselves by refusing to admit when we have done wrong. We ignore psychology's fundamental law: the need to confess.

WE NEED TO CONFESS

This need to confess, says psychologist Paul Johnson, "is one of the imperatives for health of soul."

Some years ago I was in my study preparing a sermon. The phone rang. A man who sounded very agitated said he had to see me right away. I told him I would be glad to see him. In a few minutes he was at my door, pale with fright and so upset he could not sit down.

He could hardly talk because of acute nervousness. But I managed to learn that he was terrified of the wind, and the very mention of a coming storm by a local weather forecaster was enough to drive him into a frenzy of fear. That's when he had called on me for help.

I read him some encouraging Bible promises and prayed for him. He left my office in a somewhat easier frame of mind. During the next few weeks of counseling, I learned the cause of his fear. He had committed adultery not once but many times, and his conscience was torturing him. Ignoring the need to confess his sin, he repressed his guilt. As a result, irrational fears began to creep up in the corners of his mind.

The man had professed to be a Christian, but he was far away from a close relationship with God. I urged him to confess. I showed him the biblical grounds for forgiveness through the death of Christ and the consequent restoration of fellowship with God he could enjoy once confession was made.

He confessed his sin and abandoned it. The irrational fears began to loosen their grip on his mind. Better still, he began to walk anew with God. And when he moved away from our community some months later, his spiritual life was in the process of restoration.

Guilt

Vitally related to confession is guilt. We experience various kinds of guilt. First is *legal guilt*, which means we have sinned against God and stand condemned, whether we *feel* that guilt or not (Rom. 3:23).

Pathological guilt is a chronic feeling of guilt, when there is no cause for it or when it has been dealt with adequately. It is the unnecessary arousing of the conscience. Pathological guilt is rooted in a mental disorder.

Felt guilt is the normal, natural reaction to having done wrong. It is normal to feel guilty when we are supposed to feel guilty. One psychologist says guilt is "the accusative sense of failure." That is, our conscience stands as our accuser and charges us with having done wrong. The pain of feeling we have done wrong prompts us to action.

Modern psychologists have identified several wrong ways of dealing with guilt. One is *repression*, which means to ignore it. Unfortunately, the conscience will not stand to be ignored.

The Healing Power of Confession

Quite often physical symptoms appear as if caused by something else, but in truth they are caused by a conscience signaling for attention.

Another negative way of dealing with guilt is *self-justification*, as in the case of the adulteress who "wipes her mouth and says, 'I've done nothing wrong'" (Prov. 30:20). This self-justifier denies her conscience by depriving it of its function. Her conscience becomes desensitized. She overwhelms it by rationalization. Clearly for anyone to live with a desensitized conscience means to live on dangerous moral ground. This kind of person wreaks havoc on other people while blithely going about unaffected by his or her own wrongdoing.

Still another negative way of handling guilt is *projection*. Projection means simply blaming others for any wrong that has been done. Adam's attempt to avoid responsibility in the words, "The woman you put here with me—she gave me some fruit from the tree, and I ate it" is an example of projection (Gen. 3:12). This is probably the most common way of dealing with guilt. To avoid responsibility in wrongdoing does indeed bring a measure of relief. Yet, while projection eases the situation temporarily, it does not resolve it. It is a form of deception that eventually catches up with us. And at any rate, we do not deceive God.

The heart of the Christian message is that freedom from guilt is mediated through the sacrifice of Jesus Christ on the cross. We can enter into the joyful experience of not having our sins remembered any more (Heb. 10:17). The voice of conscience says, "You have sinned." But the voice of God adds, "Confess it." One is negative, the other is positive. One crushes, the other is a call to deliverance and life.

Unfortunately, many people do not respond to the call to confess their sin and wrongdoing. Many of them, like Adam and Eve, hide and refuse to face the consequences. Even though

David felt guilty about his sin with Bathsheba, he waited many months before he finally confessed. Those were months of mental and emotional agony for him. A stifled conscience can lead to both physical and mental distress. That's why Dr. Paul Tournier says that confession is "the stopper which can be pulled out so that life begins to flow once again."

FIVE STEPS IN CONFESSION

Face reality. This means to take matters into hand and face the consequences, however painful they may be. Christians should be more ready than non-Christians to admit wrongdoing. And yet some psychologists claim that Christians are the most reluctant to admit they have done wrong because they feel they should not have done wrong in the first place. They can't stand to face the truth about themselves.

Be convicted. Conviction always is God's work and always represents God's reaction to our sin. Feeling convicted is the pain of feeling God's finger pressing against our hearts. Conviction carries two messages: You have done wrong, and you must do something about it.

Repent. Repentance is our response to God's conviction. Oswald Chambers says: "Repentance always brings a man to this point: I have sinned. The sure sign that God is at work is when a man says that and means it." Repentance is the feeling of grief over a wrong committed.

Confess the sin. In confession, we must "agree" with God (1 John 1:9). The word "confess" in this verse is translated from the Greek word *homologeo*, which means "to say with" or "to agree." This means we must adopt God's attitude toward our sin. We must be careful not to cheapen our confession by minimizing our sin. There are no "little white lies" or "little white sins" in God's record book. As I said earlier, when Saul

42

was caught disobeying God in the destruction of the Amalekites, he said to Samuel, "I have sinned. But please honor me before the elders of my people and before Israel" (1 Sam. 15:30). Any confession that leaves our egos satisfied and "honored" is not a genuine confession.

Let's look at some biblical examples of confession:

David was conscience-stricken after he had counted the fighting men, and he said to the LORD, "I have sinned greatly in what I have done" (2 Sam. 24:10).

Then, at the evening sacrifice, I rose from my self-abasement, with my tunic and cloak torn, and fell on my knees with my hands spread out to the LORD my God and prayed: "O my God, I am too ashamed and disgraced to lift up my face to you, my God, because our sins are higher than our heads and our guilt has reached to the heavens" (Ezra 9:5–6).

Against you, you only, have I sinned and done what is evil in your sight (Ps. 51:4).

"Let us lie down in our shame, and let our disgrace cover us. We have sinned against the LORD our God" (Jer. 3:25).

"I will set out and go back to my father and say to him: Father, I have sinned against heaven and against you. I am no longer worthy to be called your son" (Luke 15:18–19).

Notice that a common thread runs through all these confessions. Confession is more than simply acknowledging sin. It is feeling the same revulsion toward it that God feels. It is experiencing the shame and grief that we have involved ourselves in behavior that is directly opposite the character of God. This revulsion is God-given. "Thou hast chastised me, and I was chastised . . . turn thou me, and I shall be turned" (Jer. 31:18

KJV). We cannot feel shame and loathing toward our sin unless God's Spirit prompts our hearts. This is the direct opposite of cheap confession.

Once a Christian friend and I met to restore our broken relationship. Some negative feelings had arisen between us because he had spoken carelessly about our differences of opinion. Those indiscreet words resulted in pain and controversy.

As we talked, I waited for him to acknowledge his wrong and confess it. But his "confession" came out in the following way: "If *you* feel I have offended you I am sorry." There was no admission that *he* had done wrong, only a regret that *I felt* he had.

Often we relate to God this way. "God, I'm sorry you feel I've offended you. If I have, please forgive me." Obviously this doesn't get to the root of the matter. That's why revulsion of sin is a sign that we are really dealing with it. The extent to which we feel shame is the extent to which the Holy Spirit is at work in our hearts.

Be cleansed. To be cleansed is to have a catharsis, a word we get from ancient Greek mystery rites that aimed at cleansing the emotions, prejudices, and feelings until the person emerged healed from underneath. Cleansing is a result of confession and is always a sign of confession done properly.

Cleansing means that we no longer feel the pain of guilt or shame due to our sin. A change has taken place. The "crushed bones" now "rejoice" and the "joy of salvation" is now "restored" (Ps. 51:8, 12). "Groaning" now turns into "praise" (Ps. 32:3; 51:15).

Cleansing from sin means not only that God has removed our sin but that sin itself is no longer any bar to fellowship. Confession opens the door to fellowship with God by removing the hindrance that makes renewed fellowship possible. In addition the very process of sin and confession create greater sensitivity to sin, which teaches us to avoid its repetition, much as a child learns to avoid the fire by being burned.

That's why it's important for anyone dealing with a confessing person never to minimize or cheapen that person's confession. "Don't worry about it" or "Don't take this too seriously" is dangerous advice. We must let the confessor take his or her confession to the depths of the sin, for the thoroughness of the confession will lead to a thoroughness of cleansing afterward.

CONFESSION HEALS

Spiritually, confession is the basis of reconciliation. Psychologically, according to Dr. William E. Hulme in *Counseling and Theology*, confession is "that part of the counseling process in which the counselee releases through self-expression the destructive emotions within him." Confession has rich psychological, physical, and spiritual benefits for the confessor.

To the extent that sin and guilt have created the stress that has shattered the emotions and interrupted the normal process of the body, confession will bring about health and restoration of both body and emotions.

I have seen experiences of healing and restoration like this. I remember a sickly woman who came to see me. She was a bundle of tensions, fears, and irritability. Her home life was disintegrating. She constantly abraded her relationship with her husband and children by her unceasing and impossible demands.

In probing into her past, I discovered this woman's deep feeling of resentment toward her parents. It began in her early years and grew worse with time. When she became aware of this hostility, she began to feel guilty, yet she did nothing about the poisonous attitudes she harbored deep inside her heart. She became a slave to her fears and dark imaginings.

I urged her to come clean with God first, then with her parents. I explained that confession was the only route to reconciliation, health, and happiness. I pointed out that her bitter attitude was standing in the way of her relationship to God and her family.

She began to weep. Softly, hesitantly, she began to whisper a prayer of confession and contriteness. She asked God to purge the root of bitterness that had poisoned her life. She was willing to pay any price. As she prayed on, weeping quietly, she began to feel the relaxation of a hundred slave chains being cut from her spirit. Freedom and hope surged inside her. At the close of her prayer she said, "I feel so relaxed!" It was evident that she had not felt that way for years.

In the months that followed, her health, vitality, and optimism returned with considerable force. Painful though it was, she faced her offended family members. By humbly confessing her wrong, she restored the broken bridges of fellowship and acceptance. Above all, she became a strong friend and follower of Jesus Christ.

When I think of that woman's victory, I think of Paul Tournier's caveat concerning sin: "If you don't confess it, it becomes bottled up inside you and there are few greater causes of mental and nervous tension than that." His long experience as a counselor led him also to say: "A confession to another human being (as well as to God, I might add) can lift an enormous burden off your shoulders."

The psalmist David said it earlier, in fact 3,000 years ago, out of his own experience: "Blessed is he whose transgressions are forgiven, whose sins are covered. Blessed is the man whose sin the LORD does not count against him and in whose spirit is no deceit" (Ps. 32:1–2).

3

THE HEALING POWER OF

LOVE

Several years ago a Boston newspaper carried the story of Richard, a runaway child. Abused by his parents, he fled from home. Later he was placed in the New England Home for Little Wanderers. Psychologically he was a mess. He was a compulsive, overactive boy. A slight delay in mealtime might send him into raging tantrums. Trigger-tempered and violent, Richard desperately tried to keep from falling through the cracks of society.

Then Arthur and Georgia Lawton of Framingham, Massachusetts, took Richard to live with them. Their other children, also adopted, had grown and had left home. The Lawtons, who were strong Christians, were longing to show love to another needy child.

The change in Richard after he moved to his new home was remarkable. It took time, of course. A lifetime of rejection by adults and peers doesn't disappear overnight. But gradually Richard came to trust the Lawtons. Their patient, persistent kindness and modeling of a "better way" began to heal the hurts of many years. At age twelve, Richard jumped from third-grade level in school all the way to junior high. Arthur's influence caused this. Night after night he helped Richard prepare for his next day's work at school.

Strangely enough, not only did Richard begin to heal from his psychological scars as a result of this new-found love, but the Lawtons themselves entered a new period of better and healthier relationship with each other. Communication with Richard and dealing with his hurts helped them heal their own.

The story of Richard shows the healing power of love. Richard's need for love is as old as Adam's first sin; and the Lawtons' need to give love is as old as the first sign of redemption in the human heart.

WHAT IS LOVE?

To most people love is a feeling or an emotion. But if this is all love is, it is one of the most inconstant things known to human experience. Can we say that God *loves* or that He has *feelings* of love? Did He feel so warm about the world that He sent His only begotten Son? If so, what happens to those warm feelings when His "wrath" abides on the unbelieving (John 3:36 KJV)?

Since feelings (even warm ones) change continually, we must define love on a more substantial basis. In his book *The Art of Loving*, Erich Fromm defines love as "the active concern for the life and the growth of that which we love." Obviously this is not a perfect definition, but it's a working start.

The Healing Power of Love

By "active concern" Fromm means a direct, interested involvement with the welfare of others. That interest is directed toward their betterment, their well-being. While this interest certainly includes "warm feelings," as in the case of lovers or parents, it goes beyond the feelings. In applying this definition of love to God, here's what we get: For God felt so much concern for the world that He became actively involved in our spiritual welfare by sending His only begotten Son that whoever would trust in the Son would not perish but possess eternal life.

In short, God's love is an attitude of concern for our welfare, a concern that enables Him to do something about it. What God initiates out of love helps the receiver become healed and restored.

Although any definition of love will fall short, let's banish the idea that love is a gushy, syrupy sentiment as found in sudden "crushes" or infatuations. The reason we moderns live such shallow lives is because of our shallow view of love. If love is no more than a "high on Jesus" (as one man told me lately), then we mustn't wonder why we live from high to high and have nothing to sustain us in the valleys between.

Love Struggles in a Climate of Alienation

If Adam and Eve had never sinned, they still would have needed love. But their sin intensified their need of love because of the sin-caused alienation from God and others.

This alienation became evident right after Adam and Eve sinned. The opening of their eyes (Gen. 3:7) indicates the awareness of a spiritual and psychological change. Their consciences, previously dormant, sprang into action. Feelings of guilt, shame, and fear began to race through their minds. Their first instinct was to run away and hide (Gen. 3:8), which proved clearly inadequate. Next, they resorted to blame. Adam blamed Eve, thus demonstrating the distance that already had separated them. It was the first gulf between human beings and the beginning of all the gulfs that would later occur in human history.

This alienation has been the root of our problems ever since. Spiritually, men and women are out of touch with God, the very One whom they need more than any other. Psychologically, they are out of touch with other human beings, whom they need for both mental stability and social fulfillment.

Tragically, men and women are both unable and unwilling to re-establish communication with God because they fear God's control. So they are paralyzed by two separate polarities—their need for God and their unwillingness to surrender their self-hood to God. One woman said to me recently: "I'm afraid to give my life wholly to God because I don't trust Him. I'm not sure of what He will do with it."

Likewise we are unable to relate lovingly to other human beings. Because of our gripping anxieties due to sin, our attempts to relate to others are warped—filled with timidity, suspicion, and exploitation. For example, a woman in the New York Bronx slipped into a hospital and stole a baby out of an incubator. For almost a month she gave the tiny infant tender, motherly care. When the police finally caught up with her, the woman explained that she had had such an overwhelming desire to have a child of her own that she had wandered from hospital to hospital looking for an infant to steal. Surprisingly, the baby was in excellent condition, a tribute to her ardent but misplaced love. While this story illustrates aberrational love, most human love is touched with the brush of self-interest.

Listen to the popular songs of the day and you will find them saturated with feelings of loneliness and alienation. They cry out for companionship, for the human touch (mostly sexual). They plead for acceptance and love.

The Healing Power of Love

Sexual relationships today, because of their nature, have been elevated to the status of love. For many people, sexual love is the only kind of love they know. And for many people, a sexual relationship is the only kind of a relationship they can achieve. And yet, sex can be performed without love. In fact, in the name of love, sex has become one of the most prevalent ways of expressing selfishness and exploitation—as any counselor knows.

Possessiveness is another example of the perversion of love. A mother will not let her husband discipline their child because she is afraid the child will grow up to hate her. A father will not let his son follow his own career path because he wants to shape his son into his own image. A young bride becomes furiously jealous if she catches her husband talking to another woman (especially one young and beautiful). A young husband tells his young bride in a firm, meaningful voice: "When I want sex, I want it *now!*"

These actions are not love but the distortions of it. Sin infects our total personality, and it poisons our attempts to relate to others. Of course, selfless love is possible, even as charity, deeds of mercy, and genuine philanthropy are possible. But it is not the usual, ordinary way of the natural human heart. How else can all the misery of the world be explained?

That's where the story of redemption comes in. Since we don't seek God, He seeks us. Jesus Christ is the God who became a man. Through His work on Calvary He reopened the way for us to return to God. By removing our mountain of sin, Jesus made possible the reconciliation of the human race with the Father.

To receive Jesus Christ is to be reconciled to God. To be reconciled is to receive God's bounteous love in our hearts (Rom. 5:8). And to receive that love is to be able to establish love relationships without the degrading demands of our selfish nature.

Practicing Peace

A husband imbued with God's love can give his wife a better, purer love than he could give her by himself. A wife restored to fellowship with God through Jesus Christ can become a more selfless channel of love than she could apart from God. A father can give his children steadier love than simple parental love. And children who have God's love in their hearts can relate to their parents with redemptive wholeness.

This heaven-sent love bridges the alienation that painfully impacts our human relationships. It overcomes because it is the result of a right set of priorities: reconciliation with God first, then with others. It overcomes also because it gives us the power we need to become the loving people we ought to be.

However, even though we may be Christians, all loving relationships must be continually examined, purified, and strengthened in order to prevent the old selfish nature from reasserting itself and claiming its old authority. It is the *life* of love, not the *act* of love that is required. "Love is the key," says Eileen Guder, "not to get whatever we want but to become what we ought to be."

We Want To Be Loved More Than We Want To Give Love

As a result, most of us spend our lives trying to make ourselves lovable. Women cultivate their beauty. Men develop the macho image; they try to become the hero, the conqueror. Children seek to be loved by being obedient (knowing that's what their parents want) or disobedient (if that's what's required to get their parents' attention).

In trying to make ourselves lovable, we sometimes do harm. Take grandparents for example. They will knock themselves out trying to win the affection of their grandchildren, even to the point of reversing the child-raising techniques that they used on their own children. I've heard mothers say: "Look at the way my dad spoils my son! If I had behaved the way my son behaves, Dad would have whacked the daylights out of me!" What is Granddad doing? Trying to make himself lovable.

The same "look-how-lovable-I-am" technique operates on all levels of human experience. The deep yearning of the human heart is to be loved, to be included, to be part of the caring group or unit. Isolation, with its resulting loneliness, is abhorrent to the average human being. I've heard single people say: "I'd rather go hungry than be lonely."

Unfortunately, the wrong way to achieve a loving relationship is to approach it passively. "If I make myself lovable, I will be loved." Rather, love comes to those who give it away. The people who pour themselves out for others without thinking of a return will find themselves loved in return. Long ago, St. John of the Cross said: "Where there is no love, put love and you will find love."

The biblical command to love is always *active:*

Love the Lord your God with all your heart . . . . Love your neighbor as yourself (Matt. 22:37, 39).

O love the LORD, all ye his saints (Ps. 31:23 KJV).

What doth the LORD thy God require of thee, but to . . . love him (Deut. 10:12 KJV).

Love ye therefore the stranger (Deut. 10:19 KJV).

But love your enemies, do good to them (Luke 6:35).

A new command I give you: Love one another. As I have loved you, so you must love one another (John 13:34).

Let no debt remain outstanding, except the continuing debt to love one another (Rom. 13:8).

And live a life of love, just as Christ loved us (Eph. 5:2).

Practicing Peace

Love the brotherhood of believers (1 Peter 2:17).

Dear friends, let us love one another, for love comes from God. Everyone who loves has been born of God and knows God (1 John 4:7).

These requirements mean that we *can* love. The Bible never demands what is impossible to human nature. In fact, the command to love implies a decision of the will more than an appeal to the emotions.

Some years ago I was teaching the husbands-wives portion of Ephesians 5 in which I emphasized the command, "Husbands, love your wives, just as Christ loved the church." I remember saying quite strongly that the command to love our wives requires a volitional decision that is not necessarily tied to the emotional feelings we have for them. At the close of the meeting, a young husband came to me with a light of appreciation in his eyes. He said, "I agree with you wholeheartedly. In fact you just described my case exactly."

I said, "Tell me about it."

He said, "I fell in love with Susie, or thought I did. At any rate I was never quite sure about my feelings for her. But as I prayed about our relationship, I felt distinctly led of the Lord to marry her."

"That's unusual," I said.

"Yes, it is. But once I made the decision to marry her, my feelings for her grew strong and true. So we got married."

"Tell me, how are things working out now?"

"As you know," he said, "marriage is an up-and-down way of life. When I feel as if our relationship is not functioning at its best, I always fall back on that basic commitment I made at the beginning. The feelings run high and low, but the commitment stays. It has made the difference in our marriage."

As I left this young husband, I wondered to myself, *Isn't it better to build a relationship on commitment and trust rather than on feelings? Isn't this what the command to love implies? And if it works in the most intimate of relationships—marriage—why can't it work in all areas of human life?*

I know some people will say, "Life without romantic love would be dreary indeed, maybe impossible." The Bible certainly doesn't deny romantic love; in fact, it encourages it. When love is a commitment, it is built on a better foundation than shifting, changing emotions.

The fact that God commands us to love means that every person has the capability of loving. Some people's capabilities of course will be different from others. Even people afflicted with such things as Down's Syndrome, schizophrenia, or autism can still love—though perhaps in a more limited way.

Likewise, as the capability to *give* love is universal, so is the capacity to *receive* love. Again, capacities will differ according to the person. I have seen people severely handicapped by Alzheimer's disease who responded with a warm gleam in their eyes and the hint of a smile on their lips when small children came to visit them at Christmas.

A recent *Reader's Digest* article (November, 1984) depicts the power of love in the life of a severely handicapped baby boy. Born of an American serviceman and a Korean mother, the boy suffered from twelve health problems, one of them as serious as chronic pneumonia. When he was ten months old, he couldn't see, hear, or swallow (he had to be tube fed). One doctor called him a "vegetable."

He was placed in a nursing home in Texas until his father could be discharged from the service. Surrounded by elderly residents, the baby received a great deal of love and attention. Day by day they cuddled and caressed him. And he began to grow both mentally and physically.

Later a sixty-five-year-old retired man who was confined

to a wheelchair moved into the home and immediately took the little lad under his wing. He found in him someone to give his life to, someone to shower his love on. They became close friends, each one reaching for and giving the love they both desperately needed.

Even a critical illness did not break their love relationship. The elderly man nursed the boy night and day until he became well again.

Today the five-year-old youngster is in school, attending special classes. He is functioning well and gaining ground on his peers. The "vegetable" who was beyond medical help was healed by love.

Both to give love and to receive it are ministries of healing. An acute shortage of love can exist in a country as affluent as America. A psychiatrist friend once told me he had a male patient who confessed to him: "I need to be loved, even to be cuddled." Let's not be surprised. Human beings, including adults, never outlive this need to be touched and hugged. Medical doctors have demonstrated that newborn babies, though physically well fed, will withdraw into themselves if they are deprived of physical caressing.

To Love Others Means I Must Love Myself

Contrary to what many Bible teachers say, self-love doesn't begin with Christ's command: "Love your neighbor as yourself" (Mark 12:31). This commandment only obliges human beings to do what is already true of the Trinity. Jesus said to His Father: "You loved me before the creation of the world" (John 17:24; see also Matt. 3:17; Mark 1:11; Luke 3:22). On the other hand, Jesus' love for His Father is evident in His delight in doing the Father's will (Ps. 40:8; John 4:34; 5:19–20). The Holy Spirit loves both the Father and the Son as seen in His perfect obedience to their desires and plans.

The Healing Power of Love

Since God is love (1 John 4:16), it means that each member of the Trinity is love. And because all love must have an object, it follows that the members of the Trinity loved each other before creation ever existed. Self-love, then, begins with the Trinity.

Since human beings are created in the image of God, it is logical to believe they are able to love themselves. Before Eve was created, Adam had the capacity to love at least two persons, God and himself. If Adam and Eve had never sinned, they would have loved themselves—as well as all other members of the human race who sprang from them—in all pure innocence.

When sin entered, however, that self-love became defective. We still love ourselves, but now it is difficult to draw the line between healthy self-love and selfishness. Also, the balance is difficult to achieve. On the one hand there may be too little self-love resulting in a low self-image, a modern curse. On the other hand, too much self-love results in a narcissism that can lead to a wider gap between ourselves and others.

Apart from the grace of God, it is impossible to love ourselves with proper balance. Many of our neuroses come from the inability to find the equilibrium between self-esteem and concern for others. And yet we cannot love others unless we first love ourselves. Just as the Trinity loved itself first before it loved the human race, so we must accept and esteem ourselves before we can behave the same way toward others. One thing is sure: I cannot be double-minded. I cannot love others while hating myself. If so, that "love" is not really love but a highly dramatized pretense.

The start of a wholesome self-love and a genuine love of others lies in accepting in simple faith what God says of me. God never approves of my sins, but He always accepts me as a person. When I read in the Bible of His love for me, when I

realize why He sent Jesus into the world, when I comprehend
the exciting destiny He has for me as part of His redeemed
community, I can't help believing His love for me.

Healing love, then, is a matter of simply believing God.

I once counseled a young married woman who was
struggling in the morass of self-hatred. Her marriage was a
mess. She couldn't handle her children. Her friendships had
turned sour, and she was at the point of chucking it all.

I asked her bluntly, "Kathy, how do you feel about
yourself?"

Her reply was vehement, "I hate myself. I can never do
anything right. My husband thinks I'm a loser." She went on to
describe her depression and thoughts of suicide. Life was not
worth living on those terms. And I could understand how she
felt.

We opened our Bibles, and I directed her to John 3:16 for
a start. My questions were simple, as if I were dealing with a
child. "Whom does God love?"

"The world."

"Are you part of the world, Kathy?"

"Yes."

"Does God love you, then?"

"Yes, I guess so."

"If He loves you, don't you think He sees something
valuable in you, something worth the effort of redeeming you?"

"Yes, I guess so."

On it went from verse to verse. I asked simple questions,
and she furnished simple, one-word answers.

Then we came to Matthew 13, which details the parable
of the pearl of great value. I read it several times to allow the
truth to sink in. Then I said, "Kathy, what kind of a pearl did
the merchant find?"

"One of great value," she responded.

"And what did he give up to gain that one pearl?" I continued.

She was thoughtful for a moment, then said, "Everything."

With that word "everything," a new light came into her eyes. I could almost read her thoughts as she sat staring past me into space. "Everything—the cross, the pain, the nails, the anguish, the blood—everything in order to win *me*."

We prayed shortly after that. It was a new Kathy who left my office that day, perhaps not yet conquering and triumphant, but at least on the way out of the deep pit of gloom. She had come to understand that Christ valued her life more than His own. I felt a surging hope that Kathy's new image of herself would be translated into a new image of others. I believed that Kathy's new-found healing love of herself would heal others, also.

Pure Love Must Have a Pure Course

The emphasis of this chapter is that we must be loving persons if we are to enjoy full mental and spiritual health. The question is, where do I get that kind of love? In his poetic praise of love (1 Cor. 13), Paul gives no hint as to where that love can be obtained. Because of our fallen condition, our love is tainted. We need a fountain of pure love that will energize and purify us until we overcome the defectiveness of the Fall and rise to the level of love described in 1 Corinthians 13. There is only one source—Jesus Christ Himself.

In discussing God's love, the apostle John shows us both its source and its channel (1 John 4:12–21).

Love is intrinsically linked to a Person. "God is love" John tells us. This means that love is God's *nature*, not one of the characteristics of His personality. If God's very nature is love, then we may expect Him to be loving in *all* His actions, not just when He wants to be kind and gracious. Even God's *justice* is imbued with His love, as is His holiness, His wisdom, His providence, and all His other attributes.

All love stems from God. Mother love, fraternal love, filial love, and so on, are signs of God's presence—where God has been. He has left the evidence of His love behind.

A young pre-med student was visiting Latin America. There he saw a small, poorly dressed girl who was obviously underfed. A question popped into his mind, "Why doesn't God help that girl?" Then he realized that the only way God could help that girl was through *him*. A great truth dawned on him: "Love can only pass from person to person." Then he could become God's channel of love to needy people. When human love becomes selfish and cruel, we have a corruption of the love that God placed in us. Even more, sometimes our fallenness prevents love from getting out at all.

The grand scheme of redemption is to get God back into our lives as the Lord of all. This brings love back into our lives automatically. "If anyone acknowledges that Jesus is the Son of God, God lives in him and he in God" (v. 15). Because this is a true statement, the conclusion must also be true: "Whoever lives in love lives in God, and God in him" (v. 16).

Because it's possible to have God as the Lord of my life, it's also possible to have pure, untainted, unselfish, love in my life. Through this pure love, I can reach out to others, and we can be made whole. I think that's what Paul meant when He said to his Thessalonian friends: "May the Lord direct your hearts into God's love" (2 Thess. 3:5).

By faith we must establish a connection with God, which opens the spigot of God's love and sends it splashing into our hearts. God is ready, willing, and able to establish this connection. In fact that's exactly what He said: "Hope does not disappoint us, because God has poured out his love into our hearts by the Holy Spirit, whom he has given us" (Rom. 5:5).

The Healing Power of Love

Greg and Patty were newly married. Greg was a bright, young engineer with a promising future. Patty was an attractive, stately brunette who loved her husband very much. At first their marriage was wholesome and satisfying, then problems began to develop. They began with Patty's pregnancy. She began to sink into the dark valley of depression.

Greg took his young wife from one doctor to another until they landed one day in a psychiatrist's office. His diagnosis: Patty was a borderline manic-depressive. After the baby was born, Patty was so mired down in depression she had to have therapy.

Happily she recovered. But the same thing occurred with her second pregnancy. Ever after, the strain of coping with two small children kept her in and out of therapy. Greg's financial resources dwindled to nothing. He had to borrow money to keep afloat. The children's lives were frequently disrupted when they were taken to live with someone else while their mother had therapy. Church life, family devotions, normal friendships all had to be tabled because of Patty's shaky emotional health.

One day Greg came to see me. He made a startling statement: "I don't know what kind of a marriage I have," he said, "but the doctor gives me little hope that anything will change for the better. Can I face this kind of living, if need be, for the rest of my life?"

I understood his feeling of hopelessness. I understood also what he was trying to say, but I didn't voice it. I said, "Greg, I know you love Patty, but it's going to take something more than normal spousal love to keep you in the game. You're going to have to love her spiritually."

"What do you mean by that?"

"What I mean is, you love Patty now with the eyes of a husband. You're going to have to love her with the eyes of Christ if you want this marriage saved."

I could see he still did not quite understand. "Greg, the love of Jesus Christ is more than adequate to compensate for the limited love of a spouse. Spousal love can wither and die, but nothing can kill the love of Christ. I'm asking you to see Patty as Christ sees her, to love her as Christ loves her, and to sacrifice for her as Christ sacrifices for His church. You'll save not only your marriage but possibly also Patty's mental balance." In our prayer together Greg told God he would try.

Several weeks later Greg called and gave me the tentative but heartening response, "Pastor, thanks for the word about loving Patty with Christ's love. It's working."

I'm sure Greg would be the last person in the world to assume that from now on everything's going to be effortless victory. He will have to follow Paul's advice, "Just as you received Christ Jesus as Lord, continue to live in him, rooted . . . built up . . . strengthened . . . as you were taught" (Col. 2:6–7).

As veteran missionary Eric Frykenberg says, "The pull is always downward." We must always continue to *keep* in place what God *put* in place. However, the encouragement is always that God will keep working in us until the job is done (Phil. 1:6). Just as God empowered us to believe, He empowers us to continue believing. Just as He made the initial contact, He will enable us to maintain that contact by trusting in Him.

HOW DO WE LOVE OTHERS?

We must love even when the risks are high. Dr. Paul Brand, the leprosy specialist, once visited Central India as part of a medical team treating lepers. He noticed a woman physiotherapist massaging the fingers of a woman with an infected hand. Gently but persistently the doctor rubbed the hand, smiling encouragement to the patient as she did so.

The Healing Power of Love

"Shouldn't you be wearing gloves?" asked Dr. Brand. "Aren't you afraid of contracting her disease as you massage the infected skin?"

The doctor smiled and said, "It wouldn't be the same because my touch means something to her."

Here is a case of love overcoming fear. But this overcoming was not a bland, thoughtless act of naïveté. It was calculated concern. The doctor determined to show love in spite of the risk.

And that's what we must do always. The risk of fear is always there, as is the risk of rejection, mistrust, or resentment. God calculated the risk of being rejected by us, but He went ahead anyway and sent His Son to arrange for our redemption. Suppose God had been afraid?

Fear must be overcome! So must pride, anger, and indifference. These are the enemies of love and must be laid low in the dust in order to reach our goal of loving.

Love grows and thrives when we realize that we ourselves have been loved. Thomas Merton, the American mystic, makes a penetrating observation: "There is no way under the sun of making a man worthy of love, except by loving him." What this means to you and me is that inasmuch as God loves us, we are worthy of His love. This means I am of eternal value as a person, not a cosmic speck in a desolate universe. This means I have something to live for, to hope for, and to give to others who feel unloved and unwanted.

Love will come easily (or at least more easily) to me when I realize that the Supreme Being of the universe considers me to be valuable, not someone to be treated with contempt. "We love," says John, "because he first loved us" (1 John 4:19). Psychologically, when we feel prized, we prize others; when we feel loved, we love others. Spiritually, this principle works exactly the same way.

Practicing Peace

John presents one additional argument: God and love are inseparable. To know God and to walk with Him leads inevitably to becoming a loving person. "If we love one another, God lives in us and his love is made complete in us" (1 John 4:12). No matter how ringing our testimonies or well-shored up our doctrines, if we do not love others, we do not know God. One of the chief characteristics of love is bringing people—even diverse people—into unity and harmony. "And over all these virtues put on love, which binds them all together in perfect unity" (Col. 3:14). The virtues of healthy, wholesome relationships between Christians are all cemented by love. Hatred divides people, but love unites. Hatred puffs up, but love builds up. If God is truly alive in our hearts, our lives will reflect His presence by an ardent concern for all people, which in turn will bring healing to both them and ourselves.

We must "practice the presence" of love. We must develop a love sensitivity so that we instantly recognize love's absence and fill up the vacuum with love. Someone has written, "There can be no life without love and no love without sacrifice." To be unloving is to be less than human, and certainly less than Christian. If we want to avoid living the most deprived kind of human life, we'll have to learn to love. For love is not simply the icing on the cake, it is the cake itself. It is not a desirable ornament of life, it is the stuff of which life is made.

Practical Steps to Loving

1. Where there is estrangement, pray daily for the person from whom you are estranged. Praying conditions you to accept the person. Later, when the opportunity to be reconciled comes, you will be more ready for it.

2. When there is an opportunity to build a new relationship (a new neighbor, a new member of the church,

etc.), pluck up your courage and make the effort. Most of the time your effort will pay off because new people appreciate an approach made in friendliness and love.

3. Where you have been deeply hurt by someone and can't tolerate the thought of renewing the relationship in case it happens again, remember God doesn't expect you to be servile under someone else's will. He only desires that you hold no offense in your heart and that you *will* the other person's best interests. Love does not mean you must become a doormat.

4. Where resentments and ill feelings have built up over many years, ask God to heal your memories. Pray daily for yourself and your adversary. Sing the hymn in a new way:

My Jesus I love thee, I know thou art mine:
For thee all the follies of sin I resign;
To love _____ I'm bound to learn how,
If ever I loved thee, my Jesus 'tis now.

5. Where there is an opportunity to show interest, love, and kindness, take advantage of it. Write that letter, make that phone call, send that gift. Show your interest in a tangible, understandable way. And always accompany your gesture with selflessness so that the recipient will not suspiciously wonder, "What's he (she) doing this for anyway?" Be above reproach.

Love must be our goal. To attain and hold it, we must walk with Him whose name is love and whose every concern is for our purity and wholeness. We cannot walk with God without walking in love, and we cannot walk in love without loving others.

4

THE HEALING POWER OF

FORGIVENESS

In one of his wedding sermons, German pastor Dietrich Bonhoeffer advised the bride and groom: "Live together in the forgiveness of your sins, for without it no human fellowship . . . can survive." By "survive" Bonhoeffer didn't mean without forgiveness they would die *physically*. He meant they would die *spiritually*, for unforgiveness is the death of human relationships.

This fact deeply impressed me when I counseled a woman who had been married a number of years and had caught her husband in a compromising situation. She had gone on a vacation to visit her family. Returning home, she found some money missing from its special location. She asked her husband about it, innocently enough at first, but with increasing suspicion as she noticed his embarrassment. Wilting under the intense barrage of questions, the husband admitted he used the money to take another woman to dinner.

"Was he immoral with the other woman?" I asked.

"No, he wasn't. He said he wasn't and I believe him." Then she narrowed her eyes with resolution and added: "But he has hurt me—deeply. To think I couldn't trust him! So I told him, 'I was a virgin when you married me, and I'll be a virgin from now 'til the day I die!'"

I looked at her for a moment, bewildered. "But did he ask you to forgive him?" I asked.

"Yes, he did. He begged me. And I forgave him. Still he must be punished. I'll remain a virgin until my death."

At that point I felt an urge to shout at *her*. I wanted to tell her that what she had done was not forgiveness. But somehow the intensity of her feeling, the rising color of excitement in her face, and her overall agitation made me hesitate. She was a fuse set to go off.

When she left my office, she made it clear her mind was made up. I could only grieve inwardly at what I knew would be a downward-spiraling marriage. And not only would the marriage suffer but this unforgiving woman was setting herself up for a lot of mental grief and pain.

Forgiveness is not only a religious act, not only a fulfilling of the moral law, not only a command of Jesus Christ, but forgiveness is a way of life that honors God and heals our emotional wounds. Psychologist Joshua Liebman says, "Prophetic religion through the ages has stressed the need for forgiveness and tolerance . . . psychology now supplements this insight by teaching us that we can achieve inner health only through forgiveness" (*Peace of Mind*, p. 18).

And yet, despite the fact that God commands us to forgive and despite the fact that forgiveness is beneficial for our spiritual and psychological health, we Christians find it hard to forgive. David Seamands goes as far as to say that the two major causes of most emotional problems among Evangelical Christians are the failure to *receive God's forgiveness* and the failure to *give unconditional forgiveness* to other people (*Healing for Damaged Emotions*, p. 29). My many years of pastoral experience definitely confirm this fact!

WHY DON'T WE FORGIVE?

Why is it so hard for us Christians to forgive? I'd like to suggest some possible reasons why we don't live lives of forgiveness.

We treat forgiveness as a doctrine, not a way of life. My observation of Christians and their attitude toward forgiveness leads me to conclude that a lot of us see forgiveness as *academic*, not *realized.* That is, we see it as a beautiful theory, but we're unwilling to make the effort to make it happen in our lives. Jesus made it clear that forgiveness has to be enmeshed in our total beings, not just in our heads or our catechism books. This is highlighted in His reply to Peter when he asked Him, "Lord, how many times shall I forgive my brother when he sins against me? Up to seven times?" Jesus answered, "I tell you, not seven times, but seventy-seven times" (Matt. 18:21--22).

Numbers don't count here. Jesus might just as well have said seven million and seventy times. The point He was stressing was that forgiveness has no limits. And in order for forgiveness to be available without limit, it has to be embedded in our way of life.

Here's how Corrie ten Boom, author of *The Hiding Place*, handled a situation with an "enemy." This incident was related to the Lausanne Congress on World Evangelism in 1974. Corrie said:

Practicing Peace

I love the Germans. There is not another country in which I work with such a great joy. Some of my best friends live in that land, but once, during a meeting some time ago, I met a lady who would not look into my eyes. I was speaking to her about what the Lord had done in my life, and it came to me that she was the nurse who had been so cruel to my sister, Betsie, when she was dying in a concentration camp during World War II.

When I recognized that lady, there came hatred and bitterness in my heart. And when I felt that, I knew I had not forgiven her.

Now, I knew that Jesus had said, "If you do not forgive those who have sinned against you, my heavenly Father will not forgive you your sins." But I said, "O Lord, I cannot, I am not able."

Then suddenly I saw it. I cashed the check of Romans 5:5, "God's love has been poured into our hearts through the Holy Spirit that has been given to us." I said, "Thank you, Lord Jesus, that You have brought into my heart God's love . . . and thank You, Father, that Your love in me is stronger than my bitterness and hatred."

The result of this surge of Holy Spirit love was reconciliation between Corrie and her former enemy.

Let's ponder for a moment what really happened to Corrie. When she became conscious of her anger against her enemy, she was immediately aware that she was reacting in the wrong way. She was neither thinking Christ nor feeling Christ. So what did she do? She set about correcting her wrong feelings by an appeal to God for power to suppress the natural life and express instead the life of God. This was a sign that Corrie was not living a textbook life. It was all real and painful, yet redemptive. This is the way God expects us all to live—and forgive.

70

The Healing Power of Forgiveness

We don't realize that being forgiven is a transforming experience. Remember the parable Jesus told about the ungracious servant? In fact, it was told to answer Peter's question about how often he should forgive another person. Jesus described how a servant owed his boss several million dollars, and when he couldn't pay, the boss pitied him and forgave the debt (Matt. 18:23–27).

Well, the same forgiven worker went out and found a friend who owed him a few dollars. He grabbed the friend by the throat and demanded to be paid. Even though his friend begged for a few days' grace, the servant wouldn't listen. Instead, he had his friend tossed into jail until he could pay up.

When the boss heard how his worker had treated his friend, he flew into a rage. "I canceled all that debt of yours because you begged me to," he said. "Shouldn't you have had mercy on your fellow servant just as I had on you?" And he had *him* tossed into prison until he came up with the money.

The primary point of the story is that the worker showed incredible ingratitude for the mercy that had been offered him. But the point, I think, goes further. The servant did not show mercy on his friend because the mercy he had received did not result in a true feeling of forgiveness. In other words, forgiveness had not become a transforming power in his life.

When forgiveness is not realized as forgiveness, its power is inoperative. If God's forgiveness doesn't dawn on me or grab me, my life will not experience transformation. Therefore I will not be able to forgive others. This is the implication of Jesus' parable. The servant didn't really believe he was forgiven, otherwise there would have been a change of feeling toward his friend who owed him so little.

So if you are having a hard time forgiving someone, ask yourself, "Have I really entered into the forgiveness God has given me?" Remember, to realize you've been forgiven is to be transformed!

Practicing Peace

The Bible always sees forgiveness as a transforming experience. Paul says: "Be kind and compassionate to one another, forgiving each other, just as in Christ God forgave you" (Eph. 4:32). I am to forgive others not because it's "nice" to do so but because *I* was forgiven and the power of that forgiveness energizes all my relationships with others. The biblical appeals to forgiveness are always on the basis of a transformed life.

The Christian life is not a life of push-button victory (although maybe it *ought* to be). But it is a transformed life, which means we are able to tune in to the feelings and thoughts of God, and we are able to tap His power to lift us out of the wrong and put us in the right.

That's why Jesus was so emphatic: "If you do not forgive men their sins, your Father will not forgive your sins" (Matt. 6:15). If I paraphrased Jesus' words, perhaps they would sound like this. "If you are able to forgive others, it's because you realize that you have been forgiven." Forgiveness to Jesus was not "let's play fair" or "let's be good sports about it" but rather something rooted in the divine nature. Transformed people are forgiving people. If not, something is wrong with their transformation.

We may have had only a casual sense of forgiveness when we became Christians. I always have been deeply impressed with the incident that happened to Jesus in the house of Simon the Pharisee (Luke 7). Simon invited Jesus to dinner, and while they were eating, a prostitute entered the home and began to shower tokens of love on Jesus: wetting His feet with her tears, wiping them with her hair, anointing His feet with perfume.

Simon was incensed at this demonstration and protested against that kind of woman for daring to enter his home and insult his guest. The air was tense with conflicting emotions— Simon's anger and the woman's love.

The Healing Power of Forgiveness

Jesus cooled things off by asking Simon a question: If a man forgave a debtor his debt of five hundred denarii and another one a debt of fifty, which one would appreciate the forgiveness more?

Simon answered correctly: "The one who had the bigger debt canceled."

Then Jesus made the application. He said, in effect, "You, Simon, a respectable man, treated me shabbily when I entered your house. But this woman, a woman of the streets, hasn't stopped pouring her affection on me because her sins, which were many, have been forgiven her."

Then Jesus emphasized His point: "Whoever has been forgiven much will show much appreciation. And whoever has had only a shallow experience of forgiveness will manifest only slight gratitude."

One of the reasons we forgive so superficially is because we ourselves feel we have been forgiven only slightly by God. Cheap forgiveness is always a sign that we have not dealt adequately with our sin. One thing is sure—we'll never rise above the level of our own experience. If we feel God forgave us casually, that's how we'll treat those who offend us.

Real forgiveness is always revolutionary. It is the result of a painful awareness: "I'm lost, and God is my only way out." It recognizes the deceits the old selfish nature will practice only to save face. It knows the inevitability of the consequences: "If I turn my life over to Christ, *things will be changed.*" Real forgiveness doesn't bother with halfway measures but expects the rooting out of everything that offends God. The truly forgiven person knows what God means when He says: "Return to me with all your heart, with fasting and weeping and mourning" (Joel 2:12).

There is a vast difference between real and casual forgiveness. Many Christians have only a superficial forgiveness, a bandaging of the wound instead of surgery. Casual forgiveness leads to casual living. And casual living leads to ignoring or putting off relationships that require reconciliation based on radical, deep forgiveness.

We feel self-conscious about accepting the free grace of God when we really would like to earn our own way. This uncomfortable dichotomy is reflected in the conversation that Dr. Paul Tournier of Switzerland had with one of his patients. After she had visited him weekly for many years, he said to her teasingly: "Here you are on your little pilgrimage to Geneva, your weekly reward!"

She quickly replied, "A reward I have not merited!"

"But we merit nothing in this world," he said.

The woman reflected on this for a moment, then with sharp insight said: "In the last resort, this wounds our self-love, this receiving of that we do not deserve. And this is why we have difficulty in accepting it. We would prefer to have merited it; we contend with God for the merit" (*Guilt and Grace*, p. 195).

The woman spoke honestly about a problem that few Evangelicals would even mention. My experience with Christian people leads me to say that many of them have an erroneous view of God's free grace.

I don't mean they don't *believe* it. I mean they are uncomfortable in making it part of their lives.

A woman once said to me, "I will not sing 'for such a worm as I.' I'm not a worm!" Another person said, "I don't believe God wants me to crawl to Him on my hands and knees. He doesn't want to crush our feeling of self-esteem."

Of course God doesn't want to crush us as *persons* (after all, He gave His Son to die for us). But on the other hand, God also will not allow us to say, "God's effort *and mine* resulted in the forgiveness of my sins." Calvary was far too cataclysmic an event to let any of us think that it is only *partially* effective. I must never conclude that God saved me because I possessed merit worthy of salvation. My worth to God is that I'm a prized, dearly loved object of salvation, not that I possess a worthiness that becomes a *means* of salvation. Now, if we can only get this matter of worthiness clear, then we can put forgiveness in its proper place.

I can easily see how this wrong view of forgiveness means that I will be wrong in my forgiveness of others. I can readily understand that if I ask God to reward me with forgiveness, I will deal with others the same way. I will expect them to meet certain conditions before I grant them forgiveness. As many married people have said to me: "Sure, I'll forgive my spouse if I am convinced that he or she is going to straighten up and fly right." This is not forgiveness—it's a compromise. When God forgives us, He doesn't bargain with us; He wipes the slate clean.

Once we adopt the correct view of God's free grace in forgiveness, what a difference it makes in our attitude toward others. And what a difference it makes in our own mental and emotional health.

Dr. John White, a Christian psychiatrist from Canada, reports on the healing of a middle-aged bachelor who suffered disabling mental and emotional problems. After treating the man for months, Dr. White decided to confront his patient on the matter of his relationship to God. The man was a nominal believer, with only hazy ideas about how he could find God's forgiveness.

"I gotta make amends," the man told White. He felt somehow that he had to earn the right to be forgiven.

"Who are you," asked White, "to feel you must add your miserable pittance to the great gift God offers you?"

These words brought the man to the point of spiritual crisis. He began to pray and cry at the same time. The prayer was not formal, but more like a childlike gush: "God, I didn't know. I'm real sorry. I didn't mean to offend you. Gee, God, thank you."

The aftermath of this decision was spiritually and medically dramatic. The man was taken off medication. Daily reports on his case indicated remarkable improvement in reduced depression and paranoia. Dr. White says: "He was practically made whole" (*The Masks of Melancholy*, pp. 15–17).

Two things in this story stand out like twin towers of a New York skyscraper. First, this ailing man couldn't accept God's forgiveness unless he felt meritorious enough to receive it, "I gotta make amends." Once he saw that God's grace was totally free, he became a humble penitent. That did it. He was (and felt) forgiven. He became infused with a fresh vitality that brought him surging health and well-being.

That's the message of this chapter. A proper acceptance of God's forgiveness not only saves our souls, but heals our emotions as well. And when we offer our forgiveness to others, we heal not only broken relationships but damaged emotions also.

FORGIVENESS HEALS

Let's examine the healing aspects of forgiveness. How do we forgive when we don't *feel* like forgiving? How can we be reconciled to someone who already has devastated us and who, we're afraid, will devastate us again?

Peter Gillquist says, "Our view of forgiveness really determines our love for God." True enough. But just as our devotion to God can become sick, weak, or faulty, so our practice of forgiveness can suffer the same way. Here are some things to consider.

The Healing Power of Forgiveness

Forgiveness Requires a New Awareness

Dr. Max Reich, the Hebrew scholar, wrote: "The best of lenses is a penitential tear." Another equally effective lens is forgiveness. The forgiver begins to see things as if for the first time. Theologian Lewis Smedes calls this new awareness "magic eyes." He says: "When you forgive someone for hurting you, you perform spiritual surgery inside your soul; you cut away the wrong that was done to you so that you can see your 'enemy' through the magic eyes that can heal your soul" (*Forgive and Forget*, p. 27).

The new awareness of forgiveness is a *discovery*. People who are able to forgive see things in themselves they have never seen before, parts of their spiritual makeup that have been touched by the magic of God's miraculous power. People who can say "I can forgive!" find themselves suddenly able to forgive. They are overwhelmed at the realization that something has happened to them they never dreamed could happen.

People who forgive others not only discover a new *self*, they discover new *others*. Their enemies have lost their ugly faces and characters, which now take on the appearances of vulnerable, needy human beings.

People who are able to forgive also discover a new understanding of God. Those who forgive others are more like God in that particular act than anything else they can do. We cannot forgive someone else without understanding how God forgives us; and we can't understand how God forgives us without becoming more like Him.

Forgiving Requires an Inflow of New Power

Dr. Leslie Weatherhead, the London pastor, said: "The idea of forgiveness is the most therapeutic idea in the world." True! And the therapy is two-pronged: it heals both the forgiver and the forgiven.

77

Practicing Peace

I like to think of a broken relationship as a Humpty-Dumpty situation. According to the nursery rhyme, Humpty Dumpty's fall was permanent. There was no hope of putting him back together again.

Our human egos are like Humpty Dumpty—easy to break, hard to mend. Human beings have no natural power to repair a broken Humpty Dumpty. I may feign forgiveness to gain a point or to get out of an embarrassing situation. But I can't really forgive unless I somehow tap into divine power. Only God can forgive, and when we forgive someone else, it's because we have tapped into God's power for that act of forgiveness. Only God can put Humpty Dumpty back together again. That's why I must turn to Him for help when I need to forgive.

Turning to God for help not only enables me to forgive and heal my enemy, but also frees God to forgive and heal me. Not only is Humpty Dumpty put back together again, *I am.*

I read some time ago of a woman in Colorado who was consumed with hatred and bitterness toward the man who had brutally killed her daughter. The man had been captured, tried, and sentenced to a long term in prison. But the grieving mother could not find it in her heart to forgive him. In fact, she burned with the kind of hate that consumed everything inside her. Everything that once had brought love, laughter, and beauty to this woman turned to the ashes of hatred. Yet all the while this woman believed in God and believed that God forgives sinners.

Eventually she began to see what destruction was being wrought inside her. It slowly dawned on her that to regain her spiritual and emotional health, she would have to come to terms with the man she despised. Begging God for help, she sent the condemned man a Bible with a message of love and forgiveness. The prisoner, whose own life was filled with hopelessness and despair, replied with a message of thanks. He said, in effect, "If you could forgive me, maybe God can do the same."

The Healing Power of Forgiveness

It was the beginning of a change that led to his becoming a born-again believer. So genuine was his conversion that he began to share Christ and His Word with his fellow inmates.

The effect on the embittered woman was just as dramatic. She reported that a great burden had rolled away from her heart, and she found wholeness and peace once again.

Forgiveness Requires Initiative

"For God so loved the world that He gave His only begotten Son." I've had my share of people problems in which I hoped the issue would just dry up and blow away. Something did dry up and blow away, but it wasn't my alienation with my friend; it was my friend! Or if he didn't exactly blow away, he became a cool, nodding acquaintance from then on. He spoke and smiled, but it was obvious his heart wasn't in it. Something precious was lost.

Also there is nothing to be gained by waiting for my "enemies" to come to *me*. The rewards of going to them are so much richer because I am identifying myself with a self-giving God, and to the extent that I copy God's actions or character I become like Him. So I must start the process if necessary.

Forgiveness Requires Willingness To Suffer Pain

Just as Jesus could not forgive us without suffering on Calvary, so we cannot become agents of forgiveness without bearing a form of pain as He did.

We're all familiar with the story of the Prodigal Son (Luke 15). We've read about the son's demand that his father give him his share of the estate so he could take off and live it up in a distant country. We remember also how the day of reckoning came, when penniless and hungry he decided to go back to his father, beg his forgiveness for the way he treated him, and try to get reestablished in the family—even if he had to become a hired hand.

The surprising part of the story is how the father welcomed his son home. And I mean *welcomed* him! There were hugs, kisses, and embraces. After this came the festive celebration dinner that was usually reserved for prominent guests. Then came the new robe, the new shoes, and the father's prize possession—the signet ring. All of this for a willful boy who had messed up his life and had embarrassed his father.

Didn't the son get off too easily? Wasn't the homecoming vastly disproportionate to his act of rebellion? Wasn't the father's forgiveness too lavishly bestowed?

Not really. What Jesus did not reveal in this story was the pain the father experienced when his son stalked out of the house. Nor did Jesus say anything about the pain and hurt of the long separation when the father's heart ached for his son, his *wayward* son. Finally, there was the pain of decision when the father, before the son ever appeared on the horizon, had to determine whether he should ever welcome the ingrate back to his arms and home again. The degree of celebration for the returning son matched the degree of victory that the father had won over his pain.

Here's the simple message of that well-loved parable: there is no sin without pain and no forgiveness without suffering. It is in the nature of things.

God suffered in the person of His Son, Jesus Christ, for the sins of the entire human race. We could not have forgiveness if God had not suffered. His suffering was infinite; His forgiveness is infinite also.

Just as God suffered in order to forgive us, we must suffer in order to forgive others. I don't mean we suffer the *penalty* of sin as Christ did. I mean we suffer *sympathetically*, as the prodigal's father hurt in his heart for the sake of his wrongheaded son or as a wife would feel the terrible pain of her husband's affair with another woman. In order for both to forgive the offender, a sort of crucifixion has to take place— someone has to die. As Dr. Paul Tournier says, "Everything must be paid for!" This means that as God took the pain of our sin on Himself, so we must take the pain on ourselves if we would be agents of forgiveness.

This is where a lot of us fail in this ministry of reconciliation. We're not willing to pay the price to become messengers of forgiveness.

We need to suffer that pain for two reasons: first, because it glorifies God; and second, because it keeps us spiritually and emotionally healthy. I'd like to examine more closely the second benefit because it deals with the theme of this book.

We must forgive others, otherwise our unforgiveness will surely damage us spiritually and emotionally. On the other hand, forgiveness is a powerful cure for many afflictions of the mind and heart. As Christians we must extrude forgiveness out of our creeds and catechisms and squeeze it into our everyday lives. Forgiveness is not a museum piece; it is a means of everyday living. It is the God-given way to restore broken relationships and keep them restored. To live forgivingly means to be ready at any given instant to repent, make amends, and take the humble position in order to rectify and remove any wrong or injury that may come between us and someone else. To ignore the opportunity to forgive is to invite brokenness. Theologian Martin Marty says: "Forgiving and being forgiven are experiences that allow me to be free for a new day."

Pastor John Huffman of Pittsburgh, Pennsylvania, tells of a parishioner who came to him one Christmas and told him he had burned with bitterness toward a fellow-businessman who had cheated him out of a substantial amount of money.

"For months now," the man said, "I have resented him,

hated him for what he's done to me and to others." He went on. "And you know, John, today I feel like a new man because yesterday I did something that's entirely out of character for me. I called him long distance to wish him and his family a merry Christmas and a happy New Year." With a brightening eye the man went on to say, "You'll never know the release that has come over me in the process."

"And that," said Pastor Huffman in retelling the story, "is the catharsis of forgiveness!"

Let me add that the healing power of forgiveness extends to the physical side of things also. Emily Gardiner Neal has written several books describing the healing power of the Lord. In one she recounts the experience of a man who had been deaf for twenty years. When this man finally forgave his son's bitter treatment of him, his forgiveness released a flood of healing power in his body, and he was cured of his deafness.

The interconnecting relationship of confession, forgiveness, and physical healing is described in the Epistle of James. "Therefore confess your sins to each other and pray for each other so that you may be healed" (James 5:16).

Just as the act of forgiveness can bring immediate physical healing, so being in a *state* of forgiveness (being a forgiving person) can prevent disease from occurring (or recurring). I think this is what Paul had in mind when he advised the Ephesians, "Be kind and compassionate to one another, forgiving each other, just as in Christ God forgave you" (Eph. 4:32). The word "forgiving" here is *charidzomai*, which means being in a state of benevolence and forgiveness. My free translation of this verse would be: "Be in a state of kindness toward each other, full of tenderness, continually forgiving one another, as God in Christ once and for all forgave you." Just as we can live in peace with one another, so we can live in forgiveness with each other. And the benefits are rich, both spiritually and physically.

The Healing Power of Forgiveness

I remember the hard-driving businessman of River Forest, Illinois, who told me at one time his feelings of resentment and hard-heartedness toward other people landed him in the hospital with a stomach full of ulcers. After surgery, he realized his drastic need for a change—change of mind, change of heart, and change of attitude toward others. His search led him to Jesus Christ, whom he accepted as Savior and Lord. He began to think differently about others. Erratic drivers were no longer cursed on the highway, and his patient, long-suffering wife was no longer tongue-lashed at home. A new, benevolent, and forgiving spirit welled up in him. He was bothered no more with ulcers.

HOW DO WE BEGIN?

What is the practical side of forgiveness? How do we initiate the process?

"How do I get started?" Ask yourself a simple question, "Am I glad God has forgiven me?" If so, don't you think you owe it to God (who had mercy on *you*) to forgive your opponents so that they may have the joy of being forgiven also? In other words, am I grateful enough for my salvation to offer the fruit of it to someone else?

"What if I don't feel like doing it?" Nowhere in the Bible are we asked to forgive on the basis of feelings. God forgives us because He is "faithful and just," not because He feels like it (1 John 1:9). Forgiveness is a choice that requires an act of will. Not to forgive is plain disobedience.

"But I've already forgiven that person once!" We are to forgive infinitely, as Jesus implied when He said to Peter, "seventy times seven" (Matt. 18:22 KJV). Forgiveness must be a way of life, not a game in which we keep score. That's how God forgives us.

Practicing Peace

"What if the other person doesn't want to be forgiven?" God never makes us responsible for the other person's decision, only for our own. As long as we forgive the other person from the heart and make the offer, God is satisfied with us, whether or not our enemy accepts our forgiveness. Beyond that, it's the *other person's* responsibility.

"The other person has hurt me too much to forgive him or her." Has your enemy hurt you any more than you once hurt Jesus Christ? Weren't you at one time God's "enemy," and didn't He willingly forgive you when you asked Him to? And further, doesn't your recalcitrance in this matter hurt Jesus every day?

"Isn't it enough to forgive the other person in my heart?" That's a good beginning, but unless your enemy *knows* you have forgiven him or her, it doesn't do much good. Further, you'll not feel the release of forgiveness until both you and your enemy know that forgiveness has at least been offered.

"What happens if I'm put down or belittled?" It's possible that if you take the initiative, your enemy might reject you. Is that any reason not to try? Think how often God is rejected every day. Does He quit offering forgiveness? Even if you do get turned off, your persistence is a sign of great godliness, because that's the way God deals with us. If rebuff comes for offering to forgive, you are suffering for Christ's sake, and therefore "the Spirit of glory and of God rests on you" (1 Peter 4:14). What better reward is there than to receive the Spirit of glory and of God?

How Do We Know That Forgiveness Has Taken Place?

We know that forgiveness has taken place when we lose the feeling of pain after forgiving. A lot of people say, "I can forgive, but I can't forget." They mean, "I'll overlook this offense, but don't expect me to get over the pain."

The Healing Power of Forgiveness

This is unreal forgiveness. Forgiveness is real, that is, it really happens when I heartily forgive my offender and as a result lose the feeling of pain that I once suffered. God doesn't expect us to *forget* the hurt, but He does expect us to *lose the sense of pain* that that hurt caused. In fact, one of the joys of forgiveness is to remember the hurt without the pain! It's just triumphant to be able to say, "Oh yes, I remember what she said to me or did to me, but it doesn't bother me anymore. We are now reconciled and at peace."

We know that forgiveness has taken place when forgiveness leads to a resumption of fellowship. When Hosea's wife, Gomer, deserted him for another man, God said to the heartbroken prophet: "Go, show your love to your wife again, though she is loved by another" (Hos. 3:1). Hosea's relationship with his wife was first strained, then broken. The final string snapped when she ran off with another man. How does a man repair that kind of a wrenching breach? God said to Hosea, "Love her as the LORD loves the Israelites" (Hos. 3:1). What a command, what an unreachable standard!

And yet Hosea obeyed. He brought erring Gomer back to his home and to himself (Hos. 3:2–3). Her coming home was the sign of full healing, complete restoration.

Ideally, all forgiveness should result in a "coming home." The past should be dealt with, the pain eliminated, the hurt removed, and the threads of the relationship picked up again. When this happens, you know forgiveness is complete, because that's the way God deals with us.

But even if forgiveness does not result in a "coming home," it is still forgiveness if: I have forgiven my offender in my heart, or if I have communicated my forgiveness to my offender so that he or she understands my forgiving state of mind. Even if forgiveness is unaccepted at that point, it is still forgiveness as far as God is concerned.

Practicing Peace

We know that forgiveness has taken place when my opponent and I can talk about the offense without feeling any pain. The first step in forgiveness is inward, that is, I forgive the other party in my heart. The second step is outward, I talk to him or her. The communication may be stilted and correct, but the fact that I'm in communication with my offender is a great step forward.

However, the greatest step forward is when I can talk to the other person about the offense itself, freely and without pain. That's when the offense is something we "remember no more" (that is, in a painful way). God remembers our sins no more (Jer. 31:34 KJV), but that doesn't mean He *forgets* them. How can an omniscient God forget anything? It means He remembers them no more *as a painful offense to Him.* Having been put away by Jesus' death on Calvary, our sins no longer represent a threat to God's holy person.

So it is with us. A tremendous advance forward occurs when my enemy and I can sit down together and talk about our injuries against each other and do it without suffering the pain. The sign of a forgiven offense is the absence of pain and hurt.

We know that forgiveness has taken place when we go forward to something better. Just as patience reaches its maturity through trouble (James 1:2–4), so Godlikeness is achieved through the practice of forgiveness (Luke 6:36). Forgiveness is never merely negative. It is designed not merely to mend breaks and ruptures in relationships but also to enable the relationship to go on to what God intended it should be.

Joseph willingly, freely forgave his brothers for what they did to him (Gen. 45:4–7). But beyond that, he provided a home for them in Egypt "to save [their] lives by a great deliverance." Thus while forgiveness was necessary, it was only a step in brotherly reconciliation and achieving the great plans of God for the nation of Israel.

The Healing Power of Forgiveness

In his book *Beyond Forgiveness*, Dr. Don Baker describes the process of discipline imposed by his church on one of the staff members who had been repeatedly immoral with women. Greg's discipline involved many steps, including breaking off all contacts with the women, confessing his sin publicly before the congregation, being relieved from all pastoral duties for twenty-six months, plus numerous other personal reconciliations with his wife, friends in the church, and so on. It was a bitterly painful episode for everyone involved. And yet when forgiveness was complete and the discipline was finished, the result was a glad restoration to ministry on the part of the once-fallen staff pastor. In his restoration message, Greg told the congregation: "Above all, I would thank God for His restorative power to make a new man of me and to allow me again the privilege of being a minister. What a glorious God we have."

Dr. Baker concludes: "With those words we concluded twenty-six of the most difficult and yet most instructive months in the life of our church family. Months of pain and perfecting. Months devoted to salvaging a worthy servant and restoring him to productive ministry" (*Beyond Forgiveness*, p. 98).

Forgiveness had done its perfect work! Forgiveness will always do its perfect work, if it is allowed. For the purpose of God in making us forgiving people is that we always climb higher and grow stronger, healed by the sheer power of forgiveness itself.

5

THE HEALING POWER OF
BELIEVING

One of the most thrilling statements of the Bible is, "For it is by grace you have been saved, through faith" (Eph. 2:8).

"Saved by faith!" What an enormous spiritual burden has been lifted from us by the truth of that simple but profound statement. No more trying to measure up. We can be delivered from our sins. We can be children of God. We can be assured of acceptance with God simply through Jesus Christ's work on Calvary.

Surely that's the best "good news" the world has ever heard. But there's more, infinitely more. The redeeming work of Christ doesn't stop with our sins; it goes on to reclaim our *personalities*. In other words, we can be psychologically and emotionally saved as well as spiritually saved. And in the same way, by faith.

Have you noticed that the qualities of the Spirit—love, joy, peace, patience, kindness, goodness, faithfulness, gentleness, and self-control—are *emotional* and *mental* qualities as much as they are *spiritual* qualities?

Josh McDowell, author of *Evidence That Demands a Verdict*, tells us that one of the greatest emotional problems of his life was his hatred of his father. It wasn't always outwardly expressed, says Josh, but it was "an inward grinding." His father was the town drunk. He was an object of scorn and derision. Josh was so ashamed of his father's drunken presence that sometimes he would tie him up in the barn to keep him from entering the house and embarrassing the family in front of visitors. Josh admits, "I even tried to poison him several times."

Now Josh's hatred was a *spiritual* problem. It was sin. But it was also a *psychological* problem because that hatred poisoned Josh's relationship with his father, his family, and others around him.

It was one thing for Josh to accept Christ as Savior and be saved from the *sin* of hatred, but could Jesus Christ also save him from the *emotional* and *psychological damage of that hatred?*

In other words, does Jesus Christ save theologically only? Or is there more?

Listen to Josh: "When I became a Christian, God's love somehow took that hatred and turned it right around to love— love so strong that I was able to look my father straight in the eye and say, 'Dad, I love you.'"

The father was bewildered. How could his son love a father like *him?* The son's answer: "Through Jesus Christ I can love you and other people as well."

That swelling love in Josh's heart caused two things to happen: it healed the emotional effects of his hatred, and it convinced his father that Jesus Christ was the answer to *his* problems, also.

The good news of the gospel is, "My righteous one will live by faith" (Heb. 10:38). To be made alive by faith means more than having our sins forgiven. It also means becoming transformed in mind, attitude, feelings, and behavior.

Dr. Lee Whiston tells the story of Dot Clark. Dot's husband Bill had several heart attacks that left her extremely anxious and worried about his condition. Each morning she would stand at the kitchen sink and watch Bill drive out of the garage, down the driveway, and out onto the highway on his way to work. As she would stand there tensely, her knuckles white as she gripped the sink, she would pray her usual daily prayer: "Dear God, please don't let Bill have another attack today."

A friend who came to visit briefly noticed how destructively anxious Dot was for her husband. Lovingly he explained to her that her fearful anxiety was radiating toward Bill, and it predisposed him to further attacks. The best thing she could do for her husband, said the friend, was to trust him entirely into God's care and relax.

It didn't happen all at once, of course, but gradually Dot learned to put Bill in God's hands. Finally the day came when she could stand at the kitchen sink without fear, watch Bill drive off to work, and pray this simple prayer: "Dear God, I place Bill in your hands today. You are with him. I thank you for caring for him. I can safely trust him to You and go about my work with a calm mind."

Bill did not have any more heart attacks. Dot's fear was replaced with faith, and both husband and wife felt the power of its warm, healing embrace (from *Are You Fun To Live With?*).

When Jesus Christ walked this earth, He used His power to cure three kinds of affliction: the spiritual, the physical, and the emotional. To a sinful man He said, "Son, your sins are forgiven" (Mark 2:5). To the physically distressed woman he said, "Daughter, your faith has healed you. Go in peace and be freed from your suffering" (Mark 5:34). To the emotionally and mentally tormented man He applied His healing power, "They saw the man who had been possessed by the legion of demons, sitting there, dressed and in his right mind" (Mark 5:15).

Is Jesus only a one-dimensional Healer? Or does He still apply that healing power in the same threefold way as He did two thousand years ago?

I say He does. He saves, He heals, He restores emotional balance as He always did. Paul confirms that emotional healing is a present component of the ministry of Christ: "For God did not give us a spirit of timidity [fear], but a spirit of power, of love and of self-discipline [sound mind]" (2 Tim. 1:7).

The common ingredient in each of the healings mentioned above was *faith*. Full of confidence in His power, the afflicted ones came to Jesus and sought to be free from their misery and distress.

WHERE DO WE GET FAITH?

Both the desire and the ability to believe are instinctive to human beings. Adam and Eve naturally trusted God in their innocent state. After we are born, we grow into natural believers because childhood is the time of rich and easy faith. Jesus alluded to this when He said, "Unless you change and become like little children, you will never enter the kingdom of heaven" (Matt. 18:3). Childhood faith, Jesus seems to say, is a pure faith. Adult faith, because it easily defects, needs to return to the faith of childhood.

Children naturally believe. That's why the English poet William Wordsworth called the child "nature's priest." Children

The Healing Power of Believing

have no difficulty believing in God and the wonderful deliverances He performs. This is the kind of faith Jesus looks for in *us*. If we want to live in the world of God's wonder, we must *believe*.

How is childlike faith nurtured? Psychologist Erik Ericson says, "The child has learned to rely on his care-givers to be there when they are needed" (*Psychology Today*, June 1983, p. 27). Ericson explains that the children first exude hope and expectation, then when their expectations get reliably fulfilled (like getting fed every time they cry), they learn to rely on the one who supplies these needs.

Childlike faith must be reinforced. Children can lose their faith just as adults can, but if their native faith is encouraged, they become typical childhood believers. In fact, they become such good believers that their view of the world becomes shaped by their faith. The world, in the eyes of the children, is made to serve them and their needs.

What happens to childhood faith when children grow up? Experience teaches us that as we grow, we begin to suffer hurt and pain. The more betrayals and disappointments we experience, the more our faith shrivels like a shrub wilted by frost. We often arrive at adulthood with only a small measure of faith in God and human beings. And by the time old age creeps up on us, suspicion instead of trust is the norm. That's why Erik Ericson says, "Real faith is a very mature attitude." In other words, it's a fairly *un*common thing for adults to have strong faith.

I vividly remember the widow who asked me to conduct the funeral service for her husband. Neither she nor her husband were churchgoers or professed any religious affiliation. But they had enjoyed a long and comparatively happy marriage, so she was devastated by his death.

After the service, when it came time to leave the cemetery,

she sobbed and wailed loudly. I tried to comfort her with Scripture, but my words meant nothing to her. I encouraged her to believe in God and trust herself to Him for the future. I remember saying to her, "You must *believe!*"

"Believe," she responded, almost with anger, "I can't believe!"

I was shaken by the vehemence of her words. I realized then (as I have noticed since) that many people have so neglected their faith that when a crisis comes, they're unable to stand against the storm.

I also am reminded of German pastor Helmut Thielicke's experience when he visited a man in the hospital. The man's mother faithfully nursed him in his final days, wrapping her warm mother-love around his dying hours. Thielicke said to her, "I admire your attitude." Her reply was, "Yes, attitude perhaps, but don't look underneath, I haven't a thing to hold on to" (*I Believe*, p. 8).

Unwittingly this woman gave an excellent definition of faith: faith is having something to hold on to—God Himself. But this woman had no such faith. She struggled through the dying and death of her son with only her mother-love to offer him—and nothing to offer herself.

As I think of these two women, I see examples of untold multitudes of people who scarcely have any faith in God at all. Their childhood faith has been shattered by the trials and frustrations of life. They are examples of what the Scottish writer Thomas Carlyle said, "Disappointment in thought and act, often repeated, gives rise to doubt, and doubt gradually settles into denial."

To attain victory, we must get back to childlike faith that expects a bottle of milk for every empty stomach and a pair of loving arms for every hurt and pain. This is not infantilism, but a quality of mind that Jesus so highly prized.

The Healing Power of Believing

Faith is *awakened in conversion.* The Bible says, "By grace you have been saved, through faith—and this not from yourselves, it is the gift of God" (Eph. 2:8).

Saving faith is not simply acknowledging Christ but, in the teen language of the day, it is to "grab" Him. It takes faith to hold on to Someone we can't see and to Whom we've entrusted our destiny.

Where can we find faith with which to embrace Christ? The Bible says, it is the gift of God. Nobody can believe *for* us, not even Christ Himself. Yet, Someone firms and strengthens the "gripping" kind of faith required to trust Christ. We are *enabled* to believe. The kind of wholehearted childlike belief, utterly sure and trusting, resurfaces out of the depth of our souls and reaches up to lay hold of the invisible Christ. The result of that embrace of faith is that we are sure, we know, and we are happy.

Saving faith, however, must be sustained and rekindled if we are to live as fully redeemed people. Many Christians acknowledge that their daily faith is not always as active or buoyant as their conversion faith. We need help in the daily exercise of faith just as we did at conversion.

Paul referred to this in Galatians: "I have been crucified with Christ and I no longer live, but Christ lives in me. The life I live in the body, I live by faith in the Son of God, who loved me and gave himself for me" (Gal. 2:20). Paul was saved by faith. He lived his Christian life by faith. His faith for daily living was exactly the same kind he needed at conversion: it was "faith in the Son of God."

A missionary to Africa realized during her first term that she did not have the faith required to keep from becoming physically and emotionally exhausted. Her tasks had become grinding labor instead of joyful offerings. She described herself as *"going without* by faith!" When the term ended, she was fed up with her Christian experience and told God she would not return to Africa until her heart was completely refilled with confidence and joy.

She spent her furlough seeking God's fullness. But as the year wore on, she only grew more restless and unhappy. Three weeks before she had to return, she attended a Bible camp in Oregon. In her own words, here's what happened:

> One day toward the close of camp I became so desperate I left the meeting and walked down the road that led to a swift-flowing little river. I stood there watching the water rush by. In anguish of heart I cried out: "O God, let all the hypocrisy, the deceit, the pride flow out of my life like this water is flowing to the sea."

> In that instant the work was done. A peace, the like of which I never dreamed existed, flooded my soul. I sat down on a big rock and worshiped my God. That was eleven years ago. Today that peace "like a river glorious" still reigns in my heart (Marian Pond, *Alliance Witness*, August 1966).

What this missionary experienced was an emotional salvation by faith. The crisis was there, the desperation, the heartfelt cry to God for help. Then came God's power that enabled her to grab hold of the resources of Christ, resources that had been there all the time but that had gone untapped because she didn't have the faith to plug into them.

God gives us these power boosts to bring us up toward the level of the faith of His Son. Jesus was full of belief. He had unbounded confidence in His heavenly Father's love and care. An indication of this is found in His prayer at the tomb of Lazarus in Bethany: "Father, I thank you that you have heard me. I knew that you always hear me, but I said this for the benefit of the people standing here" (John 11:41–42).

The Healing Power of Believing

To Jesus, it was unthinkable that the Father would *not* supply His needs, would *not* grant Him power to work miracles, would *not* provide wisdom for His teachings. In fact the only reason he prayed aloud on this occasion was not because *He* needed the assurance, but the *people* did.

Let's not excuse Jesus' vibrant faith by saying, "He was the Son of God"! Of course He was, but if you will recall how Jesus taught His disciples, you'll remember that He expected them to come up to that kind of faith also. He rebuked His disciples more for lack of belief than for anything else. He rebuked them for not having the faith to expel the demon from the boy (Mark 9). He upbraided them for being afraid in the storm on the Sea of Galilee (Luke 8). He scolded them for their tenacious doubt of the fact that He had risen from the dead (Luke 24).

Jesus taught ordinary people that simple belief in the Father's love, care, and power was expected of them. The "anxiety" section of the Sermon on the Mount is an exposition of the futility and misery of anxiety in the ordinary affairs of life. This anxiety, Jesus implies, must be displaced by faith.

What Jesus Himself *was* and what He *taught* reveal what God expects of all of us. He wants our faith strong enough for ordinary living, plus something extra for the unexpected problems or trials that may come our way. If we don't have this kind of belief, we're in for a lot of mental and emotional anguish. We must not let our faith dry up, for it's just as dangerous to live without faith as it is to live without good eyes or sound limbs. Confidence in God keeps life from coming apart at the seams.

WHAT DOES FAITH DO FOR US?

How effective is a strong faith in God? In his book *The Will to Believe*, Harvard professor William James makes a

97

forceful argument for the necessity of believing. All people believe *something*, he argues, therefore it is better to believe in God and hope for help from Him than *not* to believe in Him and find little or no help elsewhere.

James's kind of faith is very practical. He taught that not only is faith necessary for a healthy mental attitude, but it's also necessary to achieve results. He illustrates: in climbing the Alps you find yourself trapped, except for a leap across the chasm. If you believe you can make the leap, your body (nerves, muscles, etc.) will cooperate and you will make it. If, on the other hand, you doubt you can make the leap, your body will refuse to cooperate, and you will make your failure certain. To William James, faith creates the fact that it wants or, in other words, it guarantees its own success.

When I carry this kind of logic into my Christian life, however, I must be careful. Does my belief in God make Him exist? Does my faith in the Bible make it the Word of God? Obviously not. Even if I disbelieved, nothing would change the facts concerning God and the Bible. Does God cease to exist just because a percentage of the world's population does not believe in Him? The answer to that is clear.

What value then is faith? Just this. Faith is the means whereby the God who already exists becomes *my* God. Belief makes the cross of Jesus Christ the means of *my* salvation. Faith in the Bible makes it the Word of God to *me, personally*. So if I am to enter in on the full benefits of faith, I must believe, not because my belief causes these things to exist but because belief makes them my own personal possession. The full range of gospel benefits for spirit, mind, and body become my property when I believe.

The Healing Power of Believing

Faith Heals Us

Faith helps us face life's crises. Our spiritual strength or weakness is always revealed in a crisis. One night, after a busy, tiring day, I received a phone call from the city jail. The desk sergeant announced that he was calling on behalf of a young woman who wanted to talk to "the minister." Could I come down?

A few minutes later I was ushered into a cell block inside the jail and was given a seat at a small table. A young woman was brought out, pale and distressed looking. She looked hesitantly at me, then took her place uncertainly on the other side of the table.

"How can I help you?" I asked.

After a few nervous starts, she slowly unfolded her story. She was twenty-one years old. She and her young husband had recently separated, leaving her (and her young child) financially hard hit. She pleaded with her husband to help, but he had refused. With bills pouring in, she momentarily panicked and wrote a few worthless checks.

Before too many days passed, she found herself behind bars, her baby taken from her custody, and no friend to give her counsel. It was the first time in her life she had been in any such trouble. Tears of shame poured down her cheeks as she glanced around the meager room and mourned, "To think I would wind up in a place like this!"

Then she came to the point. "I want a Bible," she said. "I want to read it, study it, and live by it from now on. I don't want this to happen to me again." More tears flowed.

After she finished her story I promised to bring her a Bible. I counseled her to yield her life to Jesus Christ and rely wholly on Him. Then we prayed.

I share this story because it sharply focuses on a major

problem of many Christians. They neglect their spiritual bank account until the crisis comes, then they try quickly and desperately to fill it. The effort is often too late to prevent the damage that the crisis precipitates.

Everyone has crises. It's how we handle them that determines whether they will smash or strengthen us. The Christian has a powerful weapon that can turn crises into assets, the weapon of faith.

My mother had this kind of faith. When my father died suddenly and unexpectedly, he left a large family of ten children, half of whom were still in school. Everyone agreed that my mother was facing an awesome task.

One day a local pastor came to offer his help and support. In the midst of the conversation Mother turned to him and, looking steadfastly at him, she said: "Dr. Johnson, I am not afraid!" I'll never forget her look of determined assurance and courage. The pastor didn't forget it either, for he said to her, "I know you're not, Mrs. Evans. I know you're not!"

She had her moments of discouragement, of course. More than once I saw her break down in tears under the load of responsibility. But those were momentary stops. Faith would come surging back into her soul, and she would pick up the threads of her demanding life and forge dead ahead.

Faith imparts to us inward assurance and peace. Countless Bible verses command us to trust in God. Those same verses also reveal the *healthy effects* of trust.

Isaiah says: "You will keep in perfect peace him whose mind is steadfast, because he trusts in you" (Isa. 26:3). The underlying idea? If you will make God the object of your trust, you will enjoy *perfect* peace.

Paul echoes the same thought. "Do not be anxious about anything, but in everything, by prayer and petition, with thanksgiving, present your requests to God. And the peace of

The Healing Power of Believing

God, which transcends all understanding, will guard your hearts and your minds in Christ Jesus" (Phil. 4:6–7).

Paul urges us to take decisive action against the negative: "Do not be anxious about anything." Fearful, anxious thoughts seldom can be reasoned away. They must be rejected firmly. Then, just as decisively, we must replace our fears with positive actions like prayer and praise. What happens then? God's peace sets up a guard around the citadel to prevent the return of our defeatist thoughts and feelings. This guard is supremely effective because it is Christ's peace, not ours.

Sometimes God's healing action is *direct*. I think of the psalmist's overwhelming problems expressed in these words: "The cords of death entangled me, the anguish of the grave came upon me; I was overcome by trouble and sorrow. *Then I called on the name of the LORD: 'O LORD, save me!'* " (Ps. 116:3–4, emphasis added). Did God hear that anguished cry for help? "You have freed me from my chains" is the psalmist's answer (Ps. 116:16).

This help came directly from God, swift and to the point. No dallying around, no waiting. The laser beam of God was quickly trained on the problem, and healing occurred on the spot.

Wonderful is the joy of those who have been so helped by the Lord. And multitudes have!

But God's action is also *indirect*. He made our bodies and our minds. He knows what interferes with their smooth, vibrant operation. For some it's a virus, others a bacterial infection, others a sprain, and others a broken bone. Mentally, it may be a fear or bitterness or resentment or unforgiven sin or repressed anger or doubt or rebellion. The healing for this mental condition is *the removal of the obstacle*. God says, "Roll away the stone," and, as in the case of Lazarus, life responds by surging to a normal and healthy flow.

101

Practicing Peace

Now if we ourselves can't roll away the stone, God will help us. But let's remember that most of the time, mental and emotional healing will occur naturally when the obstacles are removed. God is still the healer, but it's indirect healing. That healing is there for the taking—if the proper conditions are met. Healthy attitudes come as a result of displacing our fears and anxieties with more dominant attitudes like love, kindness, and faith.

Have you noticed in the story of Lazarus how Jesus spent more time shoring up Martha's timid faith than He did in the actual raising of her brother (John 11)? He said to her: "Your brother will rise again." Martha interpreted this to mean Lazarus would rise at the end of the age. But Jesus made it much more personal. "I am the resurrection and the life." The emphasis was on the present tense. He was saying, "I am the Lord of life. I can turn death into life at any moment. I came to reverse the irreversible. Do you believe this?"

Martha said she did. But it was obvious that she had overestimated herself, because when the group got to the cemetery, Martha was back in Doubting Castle. She said to Jesus: "By this time there is a bad odor, for he has been dead four days!"

Almost accusingly Jesus said to her, "Did I not tell you that if you believed, you would see the glory of God?"

Four days or four seconds—what difference does it make to the Lord of life? What does impossibility have to do with Him whose very name is Almightiness? The glory of God was about to be revealed!

If you believe, Jesus says also to you, "You will see the glory of God." God can be glorified in a remitted cancer, a healed broken heart, a repaired marriage, a mind brought back to normalcy from mental anguish. Do we want to see God's *glory* in our lives? We can—if we believe.

The Healing Power of Believing

Faith imparts a conviction of power and ability. Philosopher Will Durant (1885–1981) believed that faith in God was essential to the well-being of a nation. Without faith, said Durant, a nation loses moral and spiritual fiber and simply falls apart.

The same idea was expressed by psychologist William James (1842–1910), except he applied it personally. Without faith, said James, the individual falls apart. Faith is an essential ingredient to both emotional balance and personal accomplishment.

I've often tried to put myself in the shoes of the distressed father who came to Jesus one day, asking Him to heal his demon-possessed son. "If you can do anything," he said to Jesus, "take pity on us and help us" (Mark 9).

"If you can?" responded Jesus. "Everything is possible for him who believes."

That put the responsibility right on the father's own shoulders. How would I respond if Jesus put the cure of my stricken child squarely up to my faith? Would I pass or fail?

The man must have felt that responsibility. He had a strong desire to see his son helped, but he wasn't sure about his faith. Almost in desperation he said to Jesus, "I do believe." But immediately recognizing that he was both certain and uncertain, he turned to Jesus with a feeling of helplessness and begged, "Help me overcome my unbelief!"

He had faith, but it wasn't strong. However, he was willing to commit what faith he had to Christ and ask for more. On the strength of his willingness to receive more faith, Jesus healed the man's son.

This anguished father represents us all. Is *our* faith strong enough to move mountains or heal our children? I'm sure all of us have *some* faith. Jesus can fan our feeble faith into a brighter, stronger flame until it can tackle the difficult and even the impossible.

103

Practicing Peace

Stronger faith begins with *awareness*. William James said, "Believe what is in the line of your needs, for only by such belief is the need fulfilled." That's what this father did. He didn't believe for the next day's bread, only for today's need—the need to see his son healed. And Jesus rewarded his struggling faith with more faith, until it brought the desired result.

But not all people have that kind of faith.

Scientists at the University of Pennsylvania recently discovered that rats who were given electric shocks became extremely passive. The researcher called this behavior "learned helplessness."

Those of us who deal with distressed people have learned to recognize the symptoms of learned helplessness. They characterize people who have been so beaten by life that they have given up. The result is a tragic waste of human beings made in the image of God.

When I think of this kind of a person, I think of Rick. Rick was a typical college-age dropout when he drifted into our area. No one could forget him. Hidden somewhere in the midst of blue jeans and whiskers—both unwashed—was a lost, forlorn soul.

He came to see me one day. He wanted just to "let his hair down" as he put it. "You know, Pastor," he began, "the world is tough, really tough!" Then he unfolded the story of his life, a story that depicted him as a real loser. He had been cheated out of a great deal of money. All his friends had betrayed him. Even his own family had turned against him and had written him off as a lost cause. His style of life had brought him no meaning and no rest.

I studied Rick as he slowly spun out his tale. He was a piece of flotsam and jetsam, a remnant of a life poorly directed and wastefully spent. He wound up with no faith and not too much hope. These qualities had crumbled under life's battering.

The Healing Power of Believing

I offered to help, but Rick's response was, "I gotta be goin', can't stay in one place." In a few days he disappeared like a cork on the sea, only to bob up later in some new locality trying to stay afloat.

Dr. John White says, "Unhappiness is a sign of defeat or unbelief." If so, Rick was a symbol of the lack of belief as expressed in this *reversed* reading of John's statement, "This is the defeat by which we are overcome by the world, even our *unfaith*" (1 John 5:4).

How much different the attitude of Jesus who said, "Everything is possible for him who believes" (Mark 9:23). How much different the attitude of Paul, "I can do everything through him who gives me strength" (Phil. 4:13). How much different the attitudes of those named and unnamed heroes of Hebrews 11 "who through faith conquered kingdoms, adminis-tered justice, and gained what was promised; who shut the mouths of lions, quenched the fury of the flames, and escaped the edge of the sword; whose weakness was turned to strength; and who became powerful in battle . . ." (Heb. 11:33–34).

Is it God's will for us to be defeated, discouraged, and downcast? Is it God's will for us to fret and fume over problems beyond our control? Is God in favor of our being fearful and anxious in the face of threatening events? Hasn't He made it clear in His Word that relying on Him does indeed bring relief, peace, and strength? He wants us to be happy and fruitful, and He invites us to trust Him wholeheartedly to make it happen.

I'm always refreshed when I read the biographies of Christians, especially their "victory" experiences. One of these is *Hudson Taylor's Spiritual Secret,* written by his son and daughter-in-law, Dr. and Mrs. Howard Taylor.

After many years of up-and-down Christian living, Hudson Taylor finally grasped the secret of "abiding in Christ." He began to see his relationship to Christ in a new way. He saw

105

that he was already in Christ, like a branch in the vine, therefore able to draw power and nourishment directly from Christ. Christian victory was simply letting Christ do His "natural" things in him. The idea that he was in Christ was not new to Taylor, but that he could consciously *abide* in Him made such a deep impression on him that it changed his whole way of thinking and behaving.

Taylor's discovery was not only good theology but also good psychology. He became a focused and concentrated man. He believed in the abiding life, and he believed it with all his soul. The abiding was an objective reality. His belief in the fact was the key to making the reality his own personal possession— and that's what transformed a struggling Christian into one who was consciously joyful and assured.

Taylor still had problems, but faith gave him "eagles' wings" that enabled him to handle his problems. He could now cope because of the coping power of faith that gutted his problems and left them powerless. The result was an assured, confident man.

How Can We Strengthen Our Faith?

We must visualize what we'd like to become. Do you want stronger faith, more love, a confident spirit? All right, visualize it. See it. "Faith," we read, "is being sure of what we hope for and certain of what we do not see" (Heb. 11:1). By faith we must see the invisible just as a telescope sees a ship on the horizon when the natural eye can't see it. For the work of faith is to materialize what is not material; to bring into reality what is invisible. Unless we have an idea of the kind of person we want to become, it will be impossible to move toward it.

This is what the psychologist calls "imaging." On a psychological level, imaging is "seeing the ideal," then encouraging ourselves to bring it to reality. Spiritually, imaging is seeing the kind of victorious Christians we want to be, then trusting God's power to bring it to realization. Of course imaging has its dangers and can be used for devious practices as well as holy ones. The Bible calls these "vain imaginations" (Rom. 1:21 KJV). The difference is in the intent. Imaging evil is soundly condemned by Scripture, but imaging the better person we might be is a fulfillment of Paul's expansive description of the believer: "And we, who with unveiled faces all reflect [image] the Lord's glory, are being transformed into his likeness with ever-increasing glory" (2 Cor. 3:18). By imaging or reflecting Christ by the power of the Holy Spirit, we are gradually transformed into the likeness of Christ.

We must persevere in prayer. We must keep asking God to make real in us what we have seen by faith. We must remind Him of the whole picture, right down to the last detail. What do we need? Health for ourselves or loved ones; money for a financial crisis; confidence to tackle a hard, demanding job; the conversion of loved ones and friends? Let's attack these problems by imaging them by faith and pursuing that image by prayer! Because faith accepts the solution as *fact*, all the beneficial results will begin to appear in us immediately.

Perseverance will lead us to adopt the "Habakkuk" stance: "But these things I plan won't happen right away. Slowly, steadily, surely, the time approaches when the vision will be fulfilled. If it seems slow, do not despair, for these things will surely come to pass. Just be patient! They will not be overdue a single day!" (Hab. 2:3 LB).

The fruit of perseverance is saying, "Yes, it's true, I can rest on that!" This kind of belief is crucial. It's the focusing of the whole mind and soul on seeing God work for His glory and our blessing. We must avoid doubt and questioning at this point.

Practicing Peace

We must praise as we wait, knowing God will not withhold any good thing from those who walk uprightly (Ps. 84:11). A happy, contented frame of mind is one of the signs that faith is beginning to work. Once faith has triumphed and the image becomes a reality, we will become, as William James once said, "consciously right, superior, and happy."

6

THE HEALING POWER OF
HOPE

W e are saved by hope" Paul says triumphantly (Rom. 8:24 KJV). But what does it mean to be saved by hope?

Theologically it means we have a strong expectation that we'll get our complete salvation when Jesus Christ returns to this earth. Psychologically it means we have a strong expectation that *here and now* we can reach our fullest potential as sons and daughters of God. This chapter deals with this psychological aspect of hope.

Dr. S. I. McMillen relates the story of his Japanese friend, David Tsutada. When Japan became involved in World War II, Tsutada was imprisoned because he was a Christian. He was placed in a prison that was a cold, damp hole filled with indescribable filth. His mere subsistence diet reduced his weight to seventy pounds. Tsutada fully expected to die in prison, and he resigned himself to it, if it was God's will.

While in prison, however, God revealed to His servant that He wanted him to start a Bible school in Japan. Tsutada worked on the many details of the school while he shivered in the blackness of the prison cell. When the war ended, he was released, and he began the work of forming the Bible school (which has since become an excellent training school for Christians in Japan) that God had laid on his heart.

Dr. Tsutada didn't let circumstances smother his spirit. He made the decision to obey God's will. Then he began to hope and trust and plan. His spirit soared over the confining walls of his prison and embraced the future. He prepared himself to do God's work even while he was still a prisoner. David Tsutada was saved by hope.

Salvation by hope is not a theory. It is a fact substantiated both inside and outside the Bible. The Bible describes how powerfully hope kept the prophet Jeremiah sane and safe during the terrible siege of Jerusalem (about 600 B.C.). "Yet this I call to mind and therefore I have hope: Because of the LORD's great love we are not consumed, for his compassions never fail. They are new every morning; great is your faithfulness. I say to myself, 'The LORD is my portion; therefore I will wait for him.' The LORD is good to those whose hope is in him, to the one who seeks him" (Lam. 3:21–25).

Jeremiah discovered, as we all do in time, that life exists in a tension between being consumed by our problems or consuming them by faith and hope in God. When "being consumed" gains the ascendancy, we grow depressed and despairing. However, when hope takes hold and gains control, we become confident, assured, and expectant of victory.

Another biblical example of hope is the unnamed woman

The Healing Power of Hope

who had an unchecked bleeding problem that lasted for about twelve years. The woman was most discouraged because "no one could heal her" (Luke 8). This woman elbowed her way into the surging crowd that swirled around Jesus in Capernaum as He made His way to the house of Jairus to heal his dying daughter. Unable to reach Jesus Himself, the woman stretched through the packed mob and managed to touch the edge of His cloak. When she did so, her bleeding stopped.

What were this woman's feelings as she tried to reach Jesus? She must have experienced many kinds of feelings, but one thing stands out—she undoubtedly was filled with hope.

Personally, I believe it was hope that pulled her out of the house that day to seek out the popular and much sought after Healer. I am convinced also that it was hope that gave her the nerve to push ahead when she saw how impossible it was to get close to Jesus in that crowd. I feel certain it was hope that gave her the extra strength to buck the throng and reach forth with her mightiest effort to touch the edge of Jesus' robe. And immediately, she was healed! After twelve long years!

I must admit perhaps other influences also urged this woman on that day. She must have felt desperation; she had to do something. No doubt also she had heard enough about Jesus to convince her that He was someone extraordinary. And no doubt she had concluded that she had no one else to turn to. But I believe the biggest factor of all was her *hope*.

When we think about hope, we must understand that it is a human quality, not necessarily a spiritual one. Hope, like money, is neutral. It's how we use it that determines whether its influence will be selfish or godly. A thief may hope to rob a bank while a Christian may hope to become more like Jesus. The Bible encourages Christians to hope in God or in God's Word. This is the spiritual expression of hope. But a non-Christian has hopes also because it's a human thing to do.

Practicing Peace

Hope can be a *saving* quality. In his book *The Nine Hundred Days,* New York Times correspondent Harrison Salisbury describes the long three-year German siege of Leningrad during World War II. In his research Salisbury discovered the power of hope to sustain life, a fact supported by modern psychiatrists. When citizens of Leningrad lost their will to live, they invariably died—often the same day or night. On the other hand, those who survived did so because they somehow managed to maintain their hope, which kept them alive.

Dr. Elizabeth Kübler-Ross, a specialist in death and dying, affirms Salisbury's observations. So powerful is the work of hope that its presence can prolong life in cases of incurable disease.

Dr. Kübler-Ross says that her terminally ill patients, no matter how seriously ill they were, always maintained at least a sliver of hope that a miracle drug would be found in time to cure their disease. They were eager even to take experimental drugs in the hope that their disease could be checked. This hope, says Kübler-Ross, offered the patients a chance for optimism and thus kept them alive. However, as soon as that hope vanished completely and finally, they died—usually within twenty-four hours. We are indeed saved by hope.

WHAT IS HOPE?

The dictionary defines hope as "cherishing a desire with expectation of fulfillment." Another definition is, "the expectation of fulfillment or success." We can better define hope by contrasting it with similar attitudes, such as wishfulness and expectancy. To wish is to desire something. To expect is to desire something and to be relatively certain of receiving it. To hope is to desire something and to have sufficient assurance of

112

receiving it. Expanding on these definitions, we can devise a list of the ingredients in hope.

All hope must have an adequate basis. In this sense hope is like faith: it must have an adequate foundation. To pin our hopes on intuition, sentiment, or feeling is not sufficient. The reason Dr. Kübler-Ross's patients eventually died was because their flimsy foundation of hoping for a cure fell into pieces due to the lack of sufficient evidence. Our hope must be hope, not *hope so.* It must be a hope, not a *wish.*

We must not build our hope on fancies or dreams, as in Charles Dickens's book *Great Expectations,* in which Kit builds a fanciful hope that he will inherit the estate of Miss Havisham, the eccentric dowager of the town. Kit's great expectations were shattered with disappointment when he learned that not a penny from Miss Havisham came to him after her death.

Fortunately, we have a better basis than that on which to build our hope. The Bible is the basis of our hope. Paul says: "For everything that was written in the past was written to teach us, so that through endurance and the encouragement of the Scriptures we might have hope" (Rom. 15:4).

The Bible creates hope in us because it promises to help us. But even more, our hope in the Bible is strengthened because of the One who wrote those promises, the Author of the Bible. That's why God is portrayed as the God of hope (Rom. 15:13). He is the One who not only creates hope but fulfills it. Those who trust in God for their hope will never be put to shame (1 Peter 2:6). That is, God will never deceive those who base their hope on Him.

With such a solid, sure foundation, our hope in God can be a powerful healing and energizing force.

All hope must have a strong desire. The desire element in hope is always positive and hopeful. No one ever hopes for a disaster. The woman with the issue of blood had an intense desire to be healed by Jesus. Hope is not hope if it doesn't long for a desirable objective to be realized.

There is a direct relationship between hope and health. The optimistic, hopeful person has a better chance against disease, as every doctor knows. I once heard a hospital chaplain say that hopeful, trusting surgical patients survive their surgery quicker and more satisfactorily than those who feel doubtful and pessimistic.

Emotionally, no one can survive without hope. The desire to see our children grow and thrive is a powerful tonic to our own mental health. The hope of seeing prayers answered for ourselves, our families, our nation can be one of the tributaries of our emotional and mental health.

To the extent that I *purify* my hopes (that is, make them conform to God's will), *practicalize* my hopes (that is, cut them down to realizable size—no crying for the moon), and *intensify* my hopes (that is, make them serve as a powerful incentive to godly, wholesome activity), I will become a stronger person in spirit and mind.

All hope requires sufficient expectation. Expectation is not the same thing as hope. It is an *ingredient* of hope. Expectation, according to the dictionary, is "to be certain that things will happen." A pregnant woman uses the word "expect" in the correct way. She is certain that she is carrying a child and that the child eventually will be born.

That's why Christian salvation is called a "hope" (Heb. 6:18–20). We are certain, because of Christ's work on Calvary, that every believer will be saved and safe forever. Through faith we are certain this will happen, but we still "hope" for it because, though certain, it has not yet materialized for us. The pregnant woman may expect her child, but she has yet to see the little one's face.

The hemorrhaging woman's hope was so strong that it

became an expectation. Her very persistence argues for a kind of expectation that becomes a certainty. She knew Jesus would help. But until healing took place, she had to live in hope yet unfulfilled.

All hope looks forward to the future. Hope never looks backward, always forward. The hemorrhaging woman looked forward until hope became actualized in healing. Once healing took place, hope ceased because its work was done.

Hoping is always an earthly activity. Once we are in heaven, our hope will dissolve into eternal fulfillment and will exist no more. Hoping is for now. And hope always looks toward tomorrow. It is this time aspect of hope that enables it to impart so much energy to today's living.

The forward look of hope is called a "door" (Hos. 2:15). A door implies an opening, and the "door of hope" implies a pleasant, joyful expectation to come. In Israel's case, said Hosea, if the people would turn from their idolatrous practices, God would turn their sorrow into joy and weeping into a glorious new day.

The invitation to enter the door of hope is just as much for us today as it was for the Jews of Hosea's day. Whatever our sin or problem, God offers to open the door of hope if we will trust Him and enter in.

We never know when God's door of hope will open to us. Therefore, we must never give up. Deliverance may come around the next bend in the road or with the next letter in the mailbox or in the next ring of the phone.

The story is told of a French convict who had been sentenced to a life of hard labor on Devil's Island, the French penal colony. As the ship sailed from Marseilles to its destination a fire broke out below deck. The convict, a powerfully built man, was released from his chains. But instead of saving his own life first, he saved the lives of ten others. For this act of heroism his life sentence was commuted. For this doomed man, the door of hope opened suddenly and unexpectedly.

All hope encounters and overcomes obstacles. The terrified woman who approached Jesus to be healed of her bleeding was hampered by the forbidding throng that blocked her way to the Lord. But she persisted and got the victory.

We often talk about "the trial of faith," but hope has its trials, also. Take Abraham, for example. There was *no hope* for Abraham to have a son, humanly speaking. After all, hope exists only when there is a possibility of fulfillment.

But God *told* Abraham and Sarah they would have a son. Well, that put the situation on a different basis entirely. Now "against all hope, Abraham in hope believed" (Rom. 4:18). Abraham's hope was based not on biology but on God's Word. Biologically, Abraham was "dead" to having a son, but spiritually he was energized to have a son because of the Word of God. God said it, Abraham believed it, and that faith generated the hope in his heart that he would see the promise fulfilled.

The story of Abraham shows the difference between faith and hope. Faith, like expectation, sees the matter as done. Hope on the other hand does not see it as done but with the strong possibility of its being done. Faith says, the action has already happened. Hope says, not yet, but with every assurance that it will.

To arrive at that kind of assurance, however, hope must overcome all its obstacles. To "hope against hope" is to say, "In spite of hopeless circumstances, I still will hope in God." The widow who mourns her husband's death must continue to hope. The parents who grieve for their runaway son or daughter must keep hope alive. The couple who lament the loss of their home due to a fire must fight against the tendency to feel despairing.

HOW DO WE BUILD HOPE?

Hope develops when we discover the will to live. No one can live a healthy life without the will to live. Normal people show their will to live by immersing themselves in daily life, performing the activities and functions of their usual routine. They hardly think about the deeper meaning of what they do, they simply enjoy it. This is the joy of living, the *joie de vivre.* Underneath all that contentment is hope and the will to live.

Those who are sick, however, are another story. They feel sad, depressed, anxious, and sometimes despairing. They see no purpose in the monotonous round of daily tasks. They earn a salary only to exist to continue earning a salary. They get no comfort from loved ones, friends, hobbies, or work. Life has lost its meaning for them. They wonder if it's all worthwhile and frequently think of suicide. In these people, hope is nonexistent or very weak indeed.

Once hope is gone, it is difficult to continue living. One of my parishioners, an eighty-year-old cartoonist, died within thirty days of his wife's death. With the light of his life gone, he saw no reason for continuing, and though he was physically sound, he lost hope and died.

On the other hand, another elderly church member died quite suddenly of a lung embolism. I went to see his widow to help her face the future. We chatted for a moment after she answered the door, then I asked, "How do you see the future, Sarah?"

"At first," she replied, "I didn't know how I was going to get along without John. He was my life, as you know."

"Yes, I know."

"But John and I made an agreement years ago. We decided that whoever was left would spend the rest of his or her life taking care of Clarice." Clarice was their adopted daughter whose schizophrenia required hospitalization.

117

Practicing Peace

"So you see, Pastor, I have something to live for. Taking care of Clarice will be what John wanted. I'm happy that I can go on doing something for him."

"That's great! But it will be a challenge, won't it?"

"Yes. But God will help me. I trust Him for the strength I will need to do the best I can."

Although elderly at that time, Sarah went on to live for a number of years longer because she felt she was fulfilling a purpose. This is hope in practice. It's a life-giving power because it expresses the will to live.

Hope develops when we learn the meaning of life. With beaming eyes, a first grader proudly showed his mother the gold star he had earned in school. "We got these for what we do best," he explained.

"And what do you *do* best?" she inquired.

"I'm the best rester," was the pleased reply.

All of us want to be good at something. We want meaning and purpose to our existence. But often we face a roadblock in which we wonder what our life's meaning is. We ask ourselves, what does life mean to *me?*

When he was in midlife, Russia's famous novelist Leo Tolstoy used to stand in front of his mirror and ask himself, "Why do I live? What is the meaning of my life? Why am I depressed? What am I afraid of?"

This was not a social derelict speaking but a highly successful writer, a member of the nobility with vast acreages of land, a respected citizen with family connections right up to the Russian tsar himself. Yet he faced the crisis of identity and meaning. A sense of hopelessness pervaded his spirit. He was a lost soul, not only spiritually but emotionally and psychologically as well.

All of us face these crises at times. This is particularly true of people who are burdened with heavy suffering and pain and whose only ambition is to survive—somehow. For them the question is crucial: what's it all about?

It's easy to see that hopelessness is the result of not seeing meaning to our lives. The German philosopher Friedrich Nietzsche said, "He who has a *why* to live for can bear almost any *how*" [emphasis added]. Life in any form is bearable if we see purpose in it. Even death is welcome if it serves a good and helpful purpose, like soldiers dying for their country or missionaries giving their lives to offer the good news of Jesus Christ to people in other lands.

How do we learn the meaning of our lives? Where do we go to discover what our mission in life is?

Let's look at the life of Jesus to see if we can find some answers. Undoubtedly no one has ever had a sense of purpose in life as Jesus had. Undoubtedly He was highly aware of His messianic mission. But the question is, how did He become aware? I believe He became aware of it because the Father revealed it to Him. And further, I believe the Father revealed this mission to Jesus in the practical outworking of His daily life.

I don't think Jesus went around Palestine wearing a placard that read, "I am the Messiah." He revealed what He was in the things He did, the things He said, and His general influence on society.

For example, let's look at the story of the healing of the man who had been born blind (John 9). Jesus' awareness of His mission is closely bound up with the plight and healing of this man.

The story opens with a question from the disciples: "Who sinned, this man or his parents, that he was born blind?"

"Neither," was Jesus' reply. Why then was he born blind? The answer: "This happened so that the work of God might be displayed in his life."

This reply reveals an eternal principle and Jesus' connec-

119

tion with it. No suffering is meaningless, that's the principle. And Jesus' connection with it is to deal with suffering. God's glory was about to be revealed through Jesus in the healing of this man's blindness.

Of course Jesus didn't heal every blind person in Palestine. The people He did heal represented only a small fraction of the total number of sufferers of His day.

But that's not the point. The point is that whether suffering is relieved or whether it continues to infest the sufferer, it has a purpose. The blind man's ailment was to "display the glory of God." God's glory is displayed either by a burst of power that eradicates the problem or else by showing the sufferer that pain can be the means of deepening and purifying his or her character.

If I am suffering right now, I can choose to let that suffering bully me into hopelessness or despair, or I can commit it to my heavenly Father for the glory that's in it. If I let God transform my pain into a platform of His praise, I have found meaning in my suffering and therefore meaning in my life. I exist for some worthy end, which God somehow works into His eternal program. If I know the *why*, I can bear almost any *how*.

Another item that reflects Jesus' awareness of His purpose in life is His attitude toward *time*. He said, "As long as it is day, we must do the work of him who sent me. Night is coming, when no one can work" (John 9:4).

Jesus saw Himself as the Healer-Savior sent by the Father, but He also saw Himself working according to a daily schedule. I don't mean that He jotted down a list of "things to do" each morning when He woke up. He didn't need to. He trusted His Father so totally that He began each day (I believe) by putting His foot firmly down and expecting the Father would guide Him to the next step, whether to heal an afflicted child, to enlighten someone seeking answers, or to correct someone whose values had become fuzzy. In other words, Jesus trusted that *in going,* His schedule would be laid out for Him. This meant He could see purpose for every day and every step.

Does this tell us something? Don't we often miss God's purpose for us because we miss the *daily* meaning of life? Isn't it true that we often ask God to tell us what our "mission" in life is and expect to have the grandiose blueprint laid right in front of us?

No, no! God leads us as He led Jesus—step by step. Unless we can see the purpose of our living in the *minor* details, we'll probably never see it in the *major* ones.

Naturally, to see purpose in the minor details takes faith. Jesus had that faith and so can we. We need to see that in the humdrum, unexciting, plodding duties of today we can find God's purpose. In caring for a sick child, I can see I'm *needed;* in writing a cheery note to a sick friend, I can see I'm *used;* in being a loving helpmate to my appreciative spouse, I can see that I'm *praised.* It isn't long before I see that I am included in God's daily assignments.

A friend of mine went to his boss in an insurance company and announced he was leaving his job. "But why?" asked the surprised supervisor.

"Because I want to do the will of God."

Baffled, the supervisor looked at him for a moment, then asked, "But what *is* the will of God?"

And in all honesty my friend could only answer, "I don't know."

The insurance supervisor had a point. How can you do the will of God when you haven't the vaguest idea of what it is?

I'm sure some of God's servants are called by spectacular visions or special interventions of God, but most of us are called by being asked to overlay our present daily tasks with glory.

This has been done even in a concentration camp. In

World War II, one inmate of a Nazi camp found purpose to his daily living by silently promising his absent mother he would keep himself alive for her sake. He and his mother had been extremely close, so he imagined the joy he would afford her when he was finally released. He lived to be released! Thus he was able to overcome the suffocating horrors of his daily environment.

We'll defeat all hopelessness if we convince ourselves that our daily lives, however uneventful and nonstimulating, have purpose and meaning. That way we'll achieve "the full assurance of hope" (Heb. 6:11 RSV), the full enhancement of life that hope brings. And who wouldn't want *that?*

Hopelessness by definition means "without hope." Without hope we slide into discouragement, depression, and despair. This kind of an attitude is dangerous to our emotional and physical health, dangerous even to life itself. That's why hopelessness must be opposed as a mortal enemy. And that's why every encouragement that enables us to hope must be welcomed as a healing balm.

Hope develops when we fulfill our responsibilities. Psychologist Viktor Frankl says, "Being human means being conscious and being responsible." To become a hopeful, optimistic person requires a firm decision of will and a new attitude of mind.

All people who feel hopeless have at least one thing in their favor—they can choose *not* to be. To say, as some do, that hopelessness is due to circumstances is to deny that a person can rise above circumstances. If I am depressed because I'm in prison, I'm admitting that not only my body but my mind and spirit are also imprisoned by four walls. But we all know that prison walls cannot confine a human spirit.

Now Christians especially ought to be examples of people who are determined to take a hopeful stance in spite of circumstances. Paul makes this clear: "Rejoice in the Lord always. I will say it again: Rejoice! . . . Do not be anxious about anything, but in everything, by prayer and petition, with thanksgiving, present your requests to God. And the peace of God, which transcends all understanding, will guard your hearts and your minds in Christ Jesus" (Phil. 4:4, 6–7).

These words were not written by a royal prince lounging on a balcony overlooking the Tyrrhenian Sea. They were written by a prisoner, a condemned man soon to be executed for his faith in Jesus Christ. Yet, as one writer puts it, Paul didn't see mud, he saw stars. If we want emotional and spiritual health, we've got to look for the stars!

Basically, we can believe whatever we want to believe. We can believe our fears and feel anxious; we can believe our bad circumstances and feel depressed; we can believe the future is black and feel hopeless. Or we can believe God when He says that all things work together for good and feel joyful and confident. The responsibility of adopting the right attitude is *ours*.

Can we afford to commit mental suicide by assuming an attitude of hopelessness? Doesn't hopelessness say, really, that God can't help and He doesn't care? Therefore isn't hopelessness a hidden form of unbelief?

I like the ring of assurance and purpose in these words:

God has created me to do Him some definite service;
He has committed some work to me which He has not
    committed to another.
I have my mission . . . .
I am a link in a chain, a bond of connection between
    persons.
He has not created me for naught.
I shall do good. I shall do His work. I shall be an angel
    of peace,

123

Practicing Peace

A preacher of truth in my own place while not intending
    to do it—if I do but keep His commandments.
Therefore I will trust Him.

Whatever, wherever I am, I can never be thrown away.
If I am in sickness, my sickness may serve Him; in per-
    plexity, my perplexity may serve Him,
If I am in sorrow, my sorrow may serve Him.
He does nothing in vain, He knows what He is about.

    —John Henry Newman, nineteenth-century English cleric

Underlying these words is the firm foundation of hope, trust, and confidence in God. If this foundation is strong, hopelessness and despair will never topple the superstructure of my life.

If I'm suffering today, God can show me that even *now* my suffering can have meaning. "My sickness may serve Him." God is able to make me see that suffering enriches my character. I will be a better person because of my pain.

Hope develops when we give God time to heal us. Waiting takes a tremendous amount of patience. But patient waiting on God is essential in healing.

Recently I looked up all the Bible words for "hope." The Hebrew language of the Old Testament uses eleven different words for "hope," while the New Testament Greek uses only one.

One fact stood out for me as I reviewed these words—they all seem to require time. The word *mikveh*, for example, means to wait on God as a farmer would wait on the rains to fill up his pools. This requires time.

Another word, *yachal*, means to hope, to be patient. It is also translated "to wait" in several other Old Testament passages. The meaning is often interchangeable. The ideas of hoping and waiting are both brought out in Jeremiah's lament over Jerusalem's destruction and his hope that God would eventually redeem His people (Lam. 3:21–25).

Certainly this fact is clear: one of the greatest healing agents that God uses for hopelessness is *time*. For this reason Dr. John White says: "The best attitude of seriously depressed people is to quit struggling for instant happiness and to hope and quietly wait for the Lord."

Hope develops when we rebuild our trust and confidence. I realize that most despairing people are in despair because they can't trust. In fact, hopelessness is the result of a broken-down trust mechanism. So how can we expect people to trust God with their whole lives when they can't trust Him from hour to hour or minute to minute?

I think the answer here is to forget about the *giant* step of faith and start to take mini-steps of trust. Once trust has broken down, it has got to be repaired. Relearning takes time and effort. We start to trust God (strangely enough) by learning to trust other human beings. Small steps with others will lead to the healing of our trust mechanism, which then will enable us to take bigger steps of trust in God.

Find someone trustworthy. Learn to take that person's word at face value. Prove that person's faithfulness in small situations: "Will you pick up a book for me at the library?" "Will you have breakfast with me next week?" And so on. Then move on to larger things, to sharing your doubts and fears. Ask that person to pray with you. Little by little rebuild your trusting mechanism until you are able to trust God with *everything*. Once you reach the last step, your hopelessness will be practically cured.

Hope develops when we praise. As I pointed out in chapter one, praise is a magnificent healer. Praise is really an affirmation of faith. And where faith is operative, hopelessness flies away. Praise is the sunshine that banishes the shadows.

The best way to learn to praise is to make it part of the routine of your life. Margaret Clarkson, the hymn writer says: "I early learned that singing hymns and meditating on their words made mundane routines pleasant and meaningful. Hymns provided companionship in my long walks to school and in illness or solitude. When I had an exam, I would set a suitable hymn going on the turntable of my mind and relax in its strength as I worked out my paper. To this day I use hymns to help me withstand life's stresses" (*Decision,* December 1981, p. 7).

Praise is extremely effective when it is tied to the common, everyday tasks before us. It is like the "taste berry," which the African says makes everything taste sweet. Praise doesn't always change our circumstances, but it changes the way we *look* at our circumstances. After all, everything is dependent on our attitude; and if we can approach our problems, large or small, with a large dose of the sunshine of praise, we will be able to tolerate and even surmount the heaviest burdens. Dr. William James, the American psychologist, says: "Believe that life is worth living and your belief will help create the fact."

Hope develops when we center our faith on God. Sir Harry Lauder, the Scottish entertainer of a generation ago, lost a son in World War I. Disconsolate over his son's death, Lauder became possessed of a feeling of hopelessness and despair. After a long bout with his darkness, he finally began to pull out of it. Later in explaining how he survived, Sir Harry said: "I realized I had three alternatives—I could take my own life, I could drown my sorrows in alcohol, or I could turn to God. And I found God."

God is the answer to hopelessness because He is the only Person who is big enough to create meaning out of chaos. He has the means to do this; He has the power, the wisdom, and

126

the loving concern necessary for the job. A suffering Christian said to me lately, "I don't know how unbelievers can exist without God." In other words, no God, no hope.

Leo Tolstoy also found this to be true. In his book *A Confession*, Tolstoy records how during a midlife despair, he went for a walk through the woods. He felt despairing because he needed God yet couldn't find Him. He shouted to the trees: "Lord, have mercy, save me!" Suddenly, Someone stood by Tolstoy's side, and Tolstoy knew it was God. His search was over. "He exists!" he shouted ecstatically, as the awareness of God's personal presence overwhelmed him with joy.

From then on Tolstoy was God's man. He labored among the poor and oppressed as a co-worker with God. He gave away his money and possessions. He signed away the rights to his publications, leaving them free for the people to enjoy. He had found the meaning of his life.

Only God can be both the source and fulfillment of our hope. "The God of hope" (Rom. 15:13) is not a name that God uses casually. The God who created us, who redeemed us, who works all things according to the counsel of His will, and who loves us with an everlasting love, says to us: " 'For I know the plans I have for you,' declares the LORD, 'plans to prosper you and not to harm you, plans to give you *hope and a future*' " (Jer. 29:11, emphasis added).

7

THE HEALING POWER OF
PRAYER

The teenager sat munching his breakfast in the breakfast nook when he heard his mother emerge from her bedroom. He knew what she had been doing. It was her habit to fix his breakfast before he went to school each morning, then retire to her bedroom to pray.

As she came out, her cheeks were wet with tears, and a soft glow filled her eyes. "Bob," she said, "what a relief it is to pray! How wonderful just to unload all your care on God and let Him hear it all. I can't tell you what prayer means to me."

The teenager murmured a "h'm," then went on eating. But he never forgot his mother's message—prayer relieves people.

Archbishop Richard C. Trench expressed the same idea in poetic form:

Practicing Peace

Lord, what a change within us one short hour
Spent in Thy presence will prevail to make—
What heavy burdens from our bosoms take,
What parched grounds refresh as with a shower!
We kneel and all around us seems to lower;
We rise, and all, the distant and the near,
Stands forth in sunny outline, brave and clear;
We kneel how weak, we rise how full of power!
Why, therefore, should we ourselves this wrong,
Or others—that we are not always strong;
That we are ever overborne with care;
That we should ever weak or heartless be,
Anxious or troubled, when with us in prayer,
And joy and strength and courage are with Thee?

Both the Archbishop and the mother said the same thing—prayer eases the burden and imparts to us a feeling of power.

This fact can be verified in so many instances. Dr. William Sadler, the Chicago psychiatrist, firmly believed in the practice of prayer, not only because he was a Christian but also because he discovered its healing powers. He said, "When we set ourselves to the work of re-collecting the scattered pieces of ourselves, we begin a task which, if carried to its natural conclusion, ultimately becomes prayer."

Sadler knew whereof he spoke. His wife, Lena, also a doctor, asked her husband to see one of her patients, a well-educated woman who was having problems with herself and her family. After several sessions of therapy with the woman, Sadler told his wife not to expect any progress because the patient had deep psychological problems. It would take a year or so to remove her "psychic slivers."

Imagine Dr. Sadler's surprise when the same woman walked into his office a few days later and announced, "My troubles are over." She had done everything Sadler had asked her to do, had overhauled her personal and family life, and had accomplished an amazing turnabout in her attitudes. When he asked the woman how she had accomplished all this in so short a time, the woman replied, "Dr. Lena taught me to pray!"

"Dr. Lena taught me to pray!" I have no doubt that this woman said her prayers before, but now she prayed. In discovering real prayer, she also discovered how to make real prayer a source of healing. She did everything that makes prayer a healing force instead of a ritual, and healing followed.

PRAYER HEALS

Prayer Heals Because It Requires Faith

The Book of Hebrews reminds us that coming to God in prayer means we have to believe He exists. "Without faith it is impossible to please God, because anyone who comes to him must believe that he exists and that he rewards those who earnestly seek him" (Heb. 11:6).

You wouldn't ask to see the president of the United States if you didn't believe such a person existed! Similarly, we pray only when initial belief in God takes place, and this belief, however tiny and incipient, is a potent power for spiritual and emotional healing.

Think of Naaman, the great war hero of Syria. He won immense fame for his military campaigns, but he had a serious, possibly fatal, physical flaw: he was a leper (2 Kings 5). His wife's handmaid, a young girl from Israel, begged her mistress to send Naaman to Elisha, the great prophet of Israel. The young girl assured her that Elisha would cure Naaman of his leprosy.

Imagine what it took for Syria's army commander to humble himself before his enemy, Israel, and submit to one of its prophets! But he did it.

Loaded with supplies, provisions, a military guard, and wealthy gifts, Naaman traveled from Damascus to Dothan, Elisha's town, and stopped at the door of Elisha's house. Naaman knew, of course, that Elisha *existed*. But to stop before his door was a sign that he believed in Elisha. It was an act of submission born of faith. He was saying, "I place myself in your hands, confident you can help me." That indeed was *faith*.

And that's the way anyone comes who approaches God in prayer *sincerely*. The very decision to come to God, plus the faith it takes to put our case in the hands of God, is often the beginning of healing.

That's why God begs us to come (Matt. 11:28). To refuse to come is to miss the promised "rest" and the joy of being healed (Ps. 30:2).

Prayer Heals Because It Requires Commitment

Commitment goes one step further than faith. Faith says, "I believe in God, and I will come to Him for help." Commitment says, "I will come to God, and I will do whatever He asks of me in order that I may be helped." Commitment is faith in action. As C. S. Lewis suggested, when we pray, Christ stands beside us to change us.

I challenged a young man on this after a youth rally in St. Louis. He sought me out after I had finished speaking and blurted out: "I don't believe there is a God!"

Startled, I searched his face to see if he was sincere. He was. I suggested that we go somewhere to talk. We found a quiet spot in a corner of the hall. "Tell me about yourself," I asked him. His university science studies had led him to reject the idea of God, so he was left with nothing on which to build his life. His life had no purpose, and he had toyed with the idea of suicide. I could see that he desperately needed and *wanted* God, but He was torn by the fear of having to surrender his intellect, which in his mind would make him an impersonal automaton, utterly dependent on God.

"Would you like to know whether or not there is a God?" I asked.

"No. I'm sure God doesn't exist." But I could see that his hunger belied his words.

"Wouldn't you like to know one way or the other?"

"How can I?" His eyes searched mine eagerly.

I opened my Bible to John 7. I read him Jesus' words, "If anyone chooses to do God's will, he will find out whether my teaching comes from God or whether I speak on my own" (John 7:17).

I explained the procedure to him. You must "do" if you want to "know." First the commitment, then the certainty.

That baffled him completely. With irritation he said, "How can I do God's will if I don't even know He exists?"

"Let's talk to God and ask Him if He exists," I replied.

That made him even more agitated. "How can I possibly pray to someone who, in my opinion, doesn't exist?"

Logically, of course, he had a point. But I pressed him, "You want to *know*, don't you?"

I could see he was struggling in a spiritual battle. To pray was to surrender, and to surrender was to lose control of his life. He gave a sigh of weariness and helplessness. He said quietly, "How do I pray?"

I said, "Pray something like this: O God, if there is a God, please reveal yourself to me."

I'll never forget that prayer. He began, "O God . . ." Then he stopped and waited for an eternity (it seemed to me). He started again, "O God . . ." Again the breakoff. This happened five or six times. Then slowly his voice changed into a melting certainty as he broke down in tears and began to thank God for hearing him and saving him. He added a prayer of surrender, yielding to the God who "didn't exist" the rights to his life.

When I left him that night, he was healed—spiritually and emotionally. With David he had prayed, "Help me, O LORD my God; save me in accordance with your love" (Ps. 109:26). Healing had come because by deciding to pray, he was actually making a commitment. He was stopping at God's door, putting himself in the hands of the One who "wasn't there." That commitment, that faith acting, brought him release and cleansing.

Prayer Heals Because It Leads to Community

The moment I pray, I'm in community with another Person—God. This means that I am immediately objectified, my problems are shared with Someone else in a way that detaches them from myself. This ends the introversion that is one of the most injurious elements of mental and emotional illness.

Emotional healing can never take place as long as we feel we cannot rid ourselves of the burden. But once we are convinced that Someone else is listening to us, Someone else cares for us, and Someone else is willing to help us, healing begins immediately. Psychologists call this action "effective transference." It means to disencumber myself of a pressing, grievous burden by spiritually transferring it to another.

Let's take this a step further. It's impossible to pray sincerely to God without becoming *aware of the needs of others*. Thus community is enlarged and to the extent that it is enlarged, the possibility of self-healing becomes even greater.

I've heard many say, "It's impossible to pray for someone else without being benefited yourself." The apostle Paul had a heightened sense of otherness in prayer. "With Paul," says Herbert Lockyer, "prayer-counsel-admonition-argument seem to flow in one silvery stream." In reading Paul's prayers for his friends (in Ephesians or Colossians), I am amazed at how much time he devoted to their deep spiritual and emotional needs. He went beyond the "bless them" and "supply their needs" kind of prayers to profound things such as knowing God and the depth of His will and love. The scope of these petitions shows me how much Paul cared for his friends and translated that concern into prayer.

Thinking of others and praying for them is a healing action. Psychotherapist Alfred Adler says: "You can be cured [from depression and other ills] in 14 days if you follow this prescription. Try to think every day how you can please someone. Make use of all the time you spend when you are unable to go to sleep by thinking of how you can please someone, and it will be a big step forward in your health" (quoted in *Reader's Digest*, April 1964, p. 227).

What better way to show love and concern for others than in prayer? That is what Jesus did: He prayed for them (John 17:9). Even now in heaven Jesus continues that ministry of otherness: He always lives to intercede for those who come to God through Him (Heb. 7:25). Of course, Jesus doesn't need healing as we do, nevertheless His example in prayer is a reminder of how we can help ourselves to better health.

Marjorie Holmes prays, "How can I ever be jealous or envious of anyone, God, so long as I remember to bless them? How can I want to hurt or wish ill to a single living soul? Blessing activates my compassion. Blessing is personal consolation when I am powerless to do more. A blessing takes no time, costs nothing. Yet it warms the heart, puts a smile on the face and a lilt in the spirit. How can I be unhappy, at least for long, when I use this dear yet simple word, 'bless'?" (*How Can I Find You, God?*, p. 124).

Practicing Peace

Swiss psychotherapist Paul Tournier tells how one woman patient abandoned her miserable ego-centered life and ministered to others. She felt she was the center of the whole world. "It is *my* accident, *my* doctors, *my* nurse, *my* injections, *my* toilet, *my* meals, *my* digestion, *my* thermometer." Then she made her decision: "I no longer wanted to be a mass of egoisms, but a living being, with a mind and heart escaping out of the prison of self."

She began to think of others. When a patient was wheeled into the operating room, she assumed a new responsibility: "To pray for the surgeon, that God would give him understanding and guide his hand surely; for the patient, that He would grant him confidence and peace; for the relatives in the garden, that they might have hope" (*The Healing of Persons*, p. 101).

The woman had found her healing. For the prayer of faith not only heals the sick one, it heals the pray-er as well! (James 5:15).

Prayer Heals Because It Allows Us to Vent Our Feelings

Prayer allows us to release our feelings to God, which is excellent therapy because it enables us to do something about our problems—unload them on Him. He has invited us to do so. "Cast all your anxiety on him because he cares for you" (1 Peter 5:7). If we believe He cares and listens with interest, our healing happens all the more quickly. Then, of course, we can't forget that God *answers* prayer, so hope is conceived and grows, which adds another powerful healing ingredient to the mix.

Recently I scanned the Bible for examples of people who vented their troubles and anxieties to God. Each prayer was prayed for different reasons, and each brought relief.

136

The Healing Power of Prayer

Give me relief from my distress; be merciful to me and hear my prayer (Ps. 4:1).

In my distress I called to the LORD; I cried to my God for help. From his temple he heard my voice (Ps. 18:6).

This poor man called, and the LORD heard him; he saved him out of all his troubles (Ps. 34:6).

But you, O Sovereign LORD, deal well with me for your name's sake; out of the goodness of your love, deliver me. For I am poor and needy, and my heart is wounded within me (Ps. 109:21–22).

In my anguish I cried to the LORD, and he answered by setting me free (Ps. 118:5).

When I called, you answered me; you made me bold and stouthearted (Ps. 138:3).

I called on your name, O LORD, from the depths of the pit. You heard my plea: "Do not close your ears to my cry for relief" (Lam. 3:55–56).

"Lord, Son of David, have mercy on me!" (Matt. 15:22).

David's prayer of confession (Ps. 51) is a venting prayer. Unwilling to own up to killing Uriah and to his sexual immorality with Uriah's wife, Bathsheba, David suffered untold agony from repressed guilt. Finally, under the coaching of God's prophet Nathan, David faced God and his own sin. He cried out to God, "Against you, you only, have I sinned and done what is evil in your sight" (Ps. 51:4). The result of this broken-hearted contrition, David knew the joy of being forgiven: "Blessed is he whose transgressions are forgiven" (Ps. 32:1). David's cry of anguish, addressed to God, had done its work. God heard and forgave. David experienced unutterable relief in the certainty of forgiveness.

Jonah's venting cry came from inside the great fish that

God had created to swallow him because he tried to run away from Him (Jonah 1–2). "In my distress I called to the LORD, and he answered me" (Jonah 2:2). In his prayer Jonah sought reconciliation with the God Whom he had offended. He called this the "sacrifice of thanksgiving." Even more, Jonah promised to renew the vow he had made to the Lord before he disobeyed (Jonah 2:9).

Jonah's sin was different from David's. David violated the moral code; Jonah rebelled against God's explicit call to service. Both sins resulted in distress of mind and heart. In both cases the men confessed their faults to the Lord and were released from their burden of guilt through forgiveness and reconciliation with God.

Hannah cried in distress to the Lord for an entirely different reason. Childless, she brought her frustrated mother's heart to God and vented her deep anguish before Him (1 Sam. 1). The old priest Eli saw her distress and assured her that God had heard. She went home in peace. Later she conceived Samuel ("God hears") and when the little boy was old enough, she brought him to Eli and gave him back to the Lord. God heard faithful Hannah's bitter, heart-rending cry. He gave her Samuel to gladden her heart. And Hannah gladdened God's heart by giving Samuel back.

Gethsemane was the venting place for Jesus. Three times Jesus entered the deep darkness of the olive trees to beg the Father to take "the cup" away from Him (Matt. 26). He shrank from becoming sin for us. He drew back from the thought of having His fellowship with the Father severed on the cross. "My Father, if it is possible, may this cup be taken from me." It was prayer of vented agony, of verbalized distress. There has never been any pain in the history of mankind like that anguish. Yet the Father could offer no relief to Jesus by *removing* the cup. The relief came in being strengthened to carry on and take the place of sinners. From that moment on, Jesus never wailed Gethsemane's prayer again. "He was heard because of his reverent submission" (Heb. 5:7).

The final example of venting is that of Paul and Silas in the Philippian jail (Acts 16). Stripped, beaten, and flogged, they were thrown into the inner cell and were fastened to the stocks (Acts 16:22–24). Obviously they felt physical pain, probably to the limit of their endurance. But even more, they felt the urge to praise God for having suffered for His name. So they "prayed and sang hymns to God" at the midnight hour.

They were relieved immediately! Perhaps the release took place inwardly while they were praying. God answered with an "Amen" and sent a strong quake that loosened their chains and tore open the doors. Eventually they were released not only from their acute pain but also from prison itself, to the further glory of God.

All of us have cried, like Peter, "Lord, save me!" (Matt. 14:30). Even people who don't enjoy a personal relationship with God pray this way. Distress prayer is the natural outcry of being human. As a boy, I prayed distress prayers to God long before I came to know Him as my heavenly Father through Jesus Christ. "To err is human," but "to pray is human" also. When a tragedy occurs, like a fire or flood or earthquake or an auto accident, we don't perform the niceties of social interaction before summoning the fire fighter or the police or the ambulance. We act swiftly because the lives of human beings are at stake.

Someone has said, "Prayer is a creature's strength—his very breath and being." This was certainly true in the above cases as well as in countless other cases throughout history.

To neglect to pray is to neglect our healing. As the old hymn reminds us:

Practicing Peace

O what peace we often forfeit,
O what needless pain we bear,
All because we do not carry
Everything to God in prayer.

Prayer Heals Because It Is a Dialogue With God

Many of us have a wrong conception of prayer. We think of it as a monologue; we view praying as "saying prayers" instead of dialoguing with God. Prayer is not talking in a vacuum, hoping God is around somewhere listening. Prayer is a dialogue, a confrontation, even a wrestling match with God, as Jacob found. A European therapist, Alphonse Maeder, says, "The practice of prayer gives us the sense of being engaged in a sort of dialogue with God."

God's interest in seeing us genuinely pray heightens His interest in us, as evidenced in the story of Ananias of Damascus (Acts 9). God told him to go visit Paul on Straight Street "for he is praying" (Acts 9:11). Paul, a devout Pharisee, had no doubt "said his prayers" religiously from his youth up. Those prayers never stirred God. But now, after his conversion on the Damascus Road, Paul was really praying, that is, dialoguing with God. God is always impressed by the two-party system of prayer!

It is the dialogue aspect of prayer—not merely saying rote, formal prayers—that brings healing. A tape recorder can be fed to reproduce rote prayers, but only a living human being can engage God in prayer on a give-and-take basis. It is this giving of oneself that brings results in prayer.

Dialogue prayer is effective because it demands purity. We cannot engage God in prayer without getting a good look at ourselves. The French writer Francois Mauriac went so far as to say, "No one can look at himself except down on his knees in the sight of God." When we dialogue with God, we become acutely aware of our impurity. Job experienced this and cried out in anguish, "Now my eyes have seen you. Therefore I despise myself and repent in dust and ashes" (Job 42:5–6).

This look at ourselves, like Job's, brings health and healing. Just as X-rays help the doctor locate a physical problem, so examining ourselves helps us see our spiritual problems that need healing. We can never be whole persons until we see what is required to make us whole. Then we can ask God for help and cleansing. The result is a relationship with God that is healthy and growing, a "normal" relationship with us as God intended it to be.

Dialogue prayer is effective because it makes us listen to God. Dr. Paul Tournier tells of one New Year's Eve when he and his wife found a new relationship with God. They both had been Christians, but they had not enjoyed a personal relationship with God.

> We were so engrossed in his service that we had scarcely any time to listen to him. We have been taught to listen to him, at length, passionately and concretely. For us this dialogue has become interwoven with our dialogue together as man and wife, imparting to it its value and its richness. From reply to reply, in spite of all our misunderstanding, all our neglect, all our running away, all our stubborn silence, it has taken us further than we imagined possible (*The Meaning of Persons*, p. 168).

The listening side of prayer is a transforming experience. Just as listening to (not merely looking at) others involves us more deeply in their lives, so listening to God involves us in who He is and what He is about. I've heard people say, complainingly, "When I pray, my words simply bounce off the ceiling. They go nowhere." The reason for this prayer failure is that we are listening to ourselves, not God. Merely throwing words at God is not praying. Praying is responding to God. Praying is hearing Him speak then responding to His message.

A good way to develop an ear for God is to take a psalm and pray that psalm as your own. Try praying the psalm out loud, inserting the personal pronouns "I" and "my" (or even your own name) into the psalm. For example, Psalm 46 can be your confidence in God when everything is falling to pieces. Or Psalm 22 can express your deep suffering. Psalm 34 can voice your despair and desire to cry out to God. Become familiar with what God is saying to you in the psalms (and other portions of the Bible) and pray out of the context of hearing God speak.

Dialogue prayer is effective because it requires harmony with God's will. To pray sincerely is to find a common ground between our wills and God's will. This common ground unites us with our infinite God and His wonderful plan for us and the whole world. This lifts us up above ourselves into purposes that are eternal. Being caught up in eternal, meaningful things exerts a healing influence on our spirits.

A Pennsylvania pastor agonized with the problem of bringing his desires into harmony with God's desires when his wife contracted "the worst kind" of cancer. With only a five percent chance that his wife might recover from a fast metastasizing carcinoma, the husband realized his desperate need of prayer.

How should he pray? That she might recover? What about other pastors' children who had been left motherless? Was his wife any better than they? Should he pray for faith? But the pastor was wise enough to know that while God *could* heal, he wasn't sure He *would*. The whole matter boiled down to two simple questions; what was God's will, and was he willing to accept God's will, regardless of its nature?

Day by day he grew more comfortable with what

The Healing Power of Prayer

Catherine Marshall calls "the prayer of relinquishment": Thy will be done. His first reaction was peace, the peace of knowing God was in charge. Then the conviction began to grow inside him that his wife would be *healed*. This conviction grew into confidence and confidence into a certainty. His peace deepened into a profound joy.

That happy, almost unbelievable day came when the doctor told them that the woman was completely free of cancer. He said to the husband, "Your wife will never die from *that* cancer." And she didn't.

This story impressed me with the direct link between the husband's prayer of submission and the woman's victory over a malignancy. Of course, praying "Thy will be done" is not uttering a magic set of words that guarantees healing. But it does guarantee *something:* an intervention of God either in healing or at least in support, strength, and blessing.

Much of our emotional, mental, and spiritual malaise is due to our resisting God's will. We are afraid of His control of us, or else we are jealous of the fact that He is *able* to control us, so we resist Him openly or secretly, by overt disobedience or by passive non-acquiescence. The solution to our condition is to pray the prayer of relinquishment.

Dialogue prayer is effective because it brings release and healing. God is bigger than we are, and He therefore is able to solve our problems and grant us peace. When the psalmist was bothered by the problem of why the wicked seemed to grow rich while the righteous languished, he rightly took his difficulty to the Lord. "When I tried [in my own efforts] to understand all this, it was oppressive to me till I entered the sanctuary of God; then I understood . . ." (Ps. 73:16–17).

How wise he was! Wisdom is not knowing all the answers, but knowing where to get them! This man, troubled by the arrogance and affluence of the wicked, went to the proper source for relief. He sought God in His house. There, under the tutorship of God as he no doubt prayed, light illumined his struggling soul and he *"understood."*

The problem was not eradicated, but it was understood. In talking about solving her problems, Marjorie Holmes says: "Prayer-eradicated? No—but at least prayer assuaged."

God does not assure every praying person that the moment the person prays all his or her problems will be solved. In fact, many problems won't be solved in this life at all. But God does promise to hear us, to understand and sympathize with us, to stand by us with encouragement and support, and to give us His strength as we need it each day. Yes, He assuages us as we pray.

And yes, He often solves the problems, too!

If prayer is as wonderful a healing power as I have described it, why don't more people pray? I believe the main reason people do not pray is because they have a faulty relationship with God. For one thing, many people don't believe in Him. By "don't believe," I mean they don't believe He is interested enough to bother with their "petty" problems and difficulties, so why bother Him?

Another reason we don't pray is because we wage war with God over what He has done or is doing to us. What He is doing, we think, bears no similarity to what we think He ought to be doing. In other words, we want to dictate to God how He ought to run our lives. How many angry-at-God people I've seen lately!

A third reason we don't pray is because we're afraid of God (as I've already hinted). We're like the little girl who, while saying her bedtime prayers one night, broke off suddenly, turned to her mother and said, "Mama, God is too much for me!" What she meant was, I'm afraid of God, He is too big, I can't handle Him. Most of us like to be able to say, "I'm in control of my life," or "I'm my own person." Translated, this means, "I'm happiest when nobody tells me what to do, not even God."

I don't intend to rebut these erroneous views of God, except just to point out that they *are* erroneous. If any of these notions gets the upper hand in our thinking, we'll never be free enough to bring our troubles to the Lord. That's why a right relationship to God is the bedrock of prayer.

But let's assume that we all want a right relationship to God through His Son, Jesus Christ. How then shall we begin to pray?

We must determine to come by a simple act of the will. Just as a counselee makes an appointment to see the counselor, so we must "make an appointment" with God, enter His presence, and bow in prayer. But we must come honestly. No counselor can help a patient who insists on hiding, covering, dodging, and evading the truth about himself or herself. So when we come to God, we must determine to come open-heartedly (nakedly, the Bible calls it) and bare our entire souls before Him.

There is no sense entering a doctor's office for help if we don't intend to follow advice. If we want God's healing, we must be willing to follow His prescription. God never gives directions so that we can consider them; He wants us to *obey* them. And, as always, we must be "instant in prayer." That is, we must learn to pray the instant we feel the need to pray, regardless of the circumstances. Prayer doesn't have to be verbal. We can pray wordlessly on a crowded bus. We should never say, "I can't wait to pray." We should *pray!*

In the final analysis, God waits for us to pray. And when He hears our groans and sighs, His parent heart delights in them as a mother delights in the sound of her child crying for help. The mother rejoices in being a mother, and God delights in being God. The help we seek will be found, as Thomas C. Clark discovered:

> Then in despair I breathed a prayer;
> The Lord of Love was standing there.

8

THE HEALING POWER OF
MEDITATION

Dr. Gerrit Verkuyl, editor of the Berkeley version of the Bible, tells of a twenty-year-old sailor named Terry, who once sat next to him on a train. Terry was raised on a Montana cattle ranch, but he never cared for the ranch or the cattle, much to his father's disappointment. He had an older brother who was an expert rancher and therefore the pride of his father's eyes. It seemed almost inevitable that the two brothers would grow to dislike each other.

At seventeen Terry couldn't wait to join the Navy. He was positively ecstatic to get away from home and be rid of the tension between his brother and himself. After a few years of service, however, Terry injured his foot. When Verkuyl found him, he was once again on the way back to his mountain home.

Practicing Peace

As the train sped over the tracks, Terry shared his enthusiasm for the Navy with Verkuyl. He showed him a picture of his battleship, pointing out its stations and indicated with his finger the "Jacob's Ladder" that hung over the side.

"Why is that rope ladder called the 'Jacob's Ladder'?" Verkuyl asked him. Terry didn't know.

But Verkuyl did.

Then, gaining Terry's interest, Verkuyl told the biblical story of Esau and Jacob, their nomadic life, their herds of cattle, and the father's preference for the older son Esau because he was adept at cattle raising and outdoor living.

He explained also how jealousy and conflict arose between the boys, how the younger lad, Jacob, ran away from home because he couldn't stand it any longer. But the farther from home he traveled, the more lonely and frightened he grew. Who really cared for him? Only his mother. His brother hated him, and his father seemed to ignore him.

Verkuyl explained that on Jacob's third night away from home, he had a strange, soul-moving experience. He dreamed of a ladder that reached all the way from earth to heaven. Angels busily climbed up and down the ladder. Suddenly God seemed to intrude into Jacob's dream with awesome presence. But the message He conveyed was comforting: God would be with him all the days of his life and would never forsake him.

"That's why," Verkuyl said to Terry, "the ship's ladder is called the 'Jacob's Ladder.'"

Terry sighed deeply. It never occurred to him that *his* story could be found in the Bible. He never realized that a man called Jacob could be like himself and that God's promise to Jacob could really be a promise to him as well.

The Bible is not only the book of *life*, it is the book of *lives*. It is not only a book from God and about God, it is also a book about human beings, for it speaks to the human condition.

Moreover, when the Bible speaks to the human condition, it speaks to the *whole* condition, not just the spiritual. The Bible addresses us as more than souls; we are addressed as complete people, who are composed of spirit, mind, and body.

Of course, our spirit (by which we relate to God) is the most important part of us; therefore the Bible gives greater prominence to the welfare of the soul. But the other two parts, the body (by which we relate to our environment) and the mind (by which we relate to ourselves and others), also receive a significant amount of attention from God because they too are necessary for us to be whole persons.

But because of sin, our wholeness is incomplete. We are, instead, broken people. The Bible, God's "Manual of Repair" for broken people, says much about our minds, our emotions, our feelings, and our attitudes. The Bible is God's appointed, powerful instrument to bring healing from spiritual and emotional distress; it is God's instrument to bring us *wholeness*.

The Bible Is a Life-giving Book

There's a great difference between the creativity of Shakespeare's writings and the life-giving power of the Bible. Shakespeare's words may snap, crackle, and pop, but they have neither power to generate life in anyone nor power to transform human nature or behavior.

The Bible does both. The reason is clearly expressed in the words of Jesus, "The words I have spoken to you are spirit and they are life" (John 6:63). Jesus didn't mean that His words were flashy, insightful, or arresting; He meant they generated life. The words of Jesus made dead people come alive, as in the case of Lazarus (John 11). When Jesus commanded the dead man to come out of the tomb, Lazarus responded because Christ's words had reinvested life into his body.

Practicing Peace

The word of the Lord caused creation to leap into existence. "By the word of the LORD were the heavens made" (Ps. 33:6). I don't claim to be a philosopher or theologian, but I understand this verse to mean that the words of the Lord are in themselves living forces of energy. Thus when God created, He simply spoke; when Jesus healed, He simply commanded; when Jesus raised people from the dead, He simply used His words to generate new life in those dead bodies. Jesus didn't consider the *damage* when He healed or restored people. It made no difference to Him whether the person was dominated by demons, shriveled in muscle tone, or physically dead altogether. His words were sufficient to reverse the damage and to restore normalcy in each case.

When it comes to the healing power of God's Word, the Bible, we must remember that it contains the same living forces. "The word of God is living and active. Sharper than any double-edged sword, it penetrates even to dividing soul and spirit, joints and marrow; it judges the thoughts and attitudes of the heart" (Heb. 4:12–13). The Bible claims for itself what no other book can: its words are *living*. And because the words are living, they can penetrate to the roots of our personalities as no other words can. There at the roots of our personalities, surgical healing can be performed by the sheer energizing force of the Word of God. The healing work of the Bible is not a papering over our deep, anguishing needs but a revitalizing of them. By the power of God's Word, homosexuals can be reclaimed to walk naturally, depressed people can be restored to serenity, guilty people can be brought to peace of conscience, fornicators can be rendered pure, thieves can be brought to repentance and restoration, hopeless people can be refurbished with optimism, and so on. This is because the Bible is "inspired," that is, "God-breathed" (2 Tim. 3:16). To be God-breathed means to be saturated with God's breath, or energy, which invests every word that He spoke. Thus when we ponder the Bible receptively, trusting the Holy Spirit to speak to our condition, we are exposing ourselves to the impulses of God's energy — impulses that are able to heal, restore, correct, and make fruitful. What an amazing healing instrument we have in our Bible!

Peter describes God's Word as imperishable seed (1 Peter 1:23). The Bible is not stalk nor blossom, both of which die. The Bible is seed that never dies. The life of the seed continues in the fruit, which produces more seed, which produces more fruit, and so on indefinitely. In his book *Why Believe the Bible*, Dr. John McArthur says: "The Word of God is the only thing we know of, apart from the Trinity itself, that is alive in the eternal sense."

Interestingly, Peter tells us that the seed of God's Word is the agent that causes us to be born again (1 Peter 1:23). In other words, the Bible is not only a living seed, it is a *life-giving* seed. By means of that life we become changed people, transformed, victorious, mature in Christ. I think this is what God means when He calls His Word the "word of life" (Phil. 2:16), that is, both *having* life and *giving* life.

The Bible Is a Power-transmitting Book

Closely associated with the Bible's life-transmitting quality is its ability to transmit *power*. This is true because of the Bible's unique Author.

One day the Lord said to Jeremiah, His prophet, "What do you see, Jeremiah?" And he answered, "The branch of an almond tree."

The Lord said, "You have seen correctly." Then He added an interesting explanation of His question, "For I am watching to see that my word is fulfilled" (Jer. 1:11–12).

What connection did an almond tree have to God's Word? The almond tree, because it budded first in the growing season, was called the "awake" tree. It heralded the new season. Explaining the analogy, God said He was always "awake" over His Word to assure its fulfillment. No human author could ever say that. No human prognosticators could guarantee that their words would unfailingly come true and that they watched over them to be sure they did.

Only God can predict something and guarantee its fulfillment. That's because He adds power to His Word to make it possible. Gabriel made this clear when he said to the Virgin Mary, "Nothing is impossible with God" (Luke 1:37). Another translation could be, "no word from God shall be without power" [author's translation].

When Jesus saw a paralyzed man near one of the pools of Bethesda in Jerusalem, He said to him, "Get up! Pick up your mat and walk" (John 5:8). This was a sharp word of command. Immediately the man was cured. Jesus' words were living impulses of energy that acted on the man's spirit, brain, and nervous system, creating vitality and wellness. Thus Jesus not only claimed His words were life, but He also demonstrated they were.

God speaks words to fulfill them, not to see them fall uselessly to the ground. He watches over His Word as a farmer watches over a seedling as it grows into fruit. God is just as much concerned about the product of His Word as a farmer is about the product of his seed. The farmer wants corn, not husks.

"Is anything too hard for the LORD?" (Gen. 18:14). The Lord asked this question of Sarah when she was told she would give birth to a son, a biological impossibility at her age. In fact, Sarah laughed at the thought. But God insisted nothing was too hard for Him. Where God speaks, sufficient power accompanies the promise to make it come true. And it did! That's why God says confidently, "My word shall not return unto me void" (Isa. 55:11 KJV).

The self-fulfilling power of God's Word is enormously important for us. It means that the hundreds of promises of the Bible can be fulfilled in us, if we meet the condition laid down for each promise.

Where the Bible promises power, we can have that power. Where the Bible promises peace, we can enjoy that peace. Where the Bible promises newness and freshness, we can experience that renewal. Where the Bible promises comfort and solace, we can be comforted. Where the Bible promises cleansing from sin and guilt, we can be cleansed and set free. Where the Bible promises wisdom and guidance, we can be guided. Where the Bible promises strength for huge tasks or strength to break an enslaving habit, we can have that strength. Where the Bible promises victory and fruitfulness, we can experience those blessings in our lives. Where the Bible promises to supply our needs, whatever they may be, we can be certain of that never-failing supply.

The Bible offers many promises to those who look to God, trust in Him, and lean hard in faith on Him. For such trusting people, God's Word indeed will not return void!

That's because God guarantees His Word.

In the early days of my ministry a team of us used to visit the "County Farm," the place where elderly, indigent people were cared for during their last years. We held regular worship services that were designed to encourage and comfort.

One day a newcomer to the facility shuffled into the room where the service was being held, and he sought me out after the service was finished. He was a small, brisk man who gave every impression of being a successful entrepreneur. "Do you need any money?" he asked eagerly as he edged up alongside me.

I looked at him. Uncertain of his purpose, I joked along
with him, "Oh sure, plenty."

"Exactly how much?" he persisted. His mood became very
businesslike.

I hesitated. I really didn't know what to say.

"Would ten thousand see you through?" he asked. Then
without waiting for an answer he drew out of his pocket a little
book the size of a checkbook and began scribbling. Then with a
benefactor's smile he placed the "check" for ten thousand dollars
in my hand! He went on his way, whistling happily.

A single glance at the "check" told me, of course, that it
was worthless. He had nothing whatever to back up his lavish
largesse, so he could write any amount he wanted, make any
promise he deemed suitable. Well intentioned as the kindly old
man was, his word and signature were without power.

I've often thought about that genial but deluded man.
Aren't many of the promises we've come to expect in life
worthless? A psychotherapist can diagnose an emotional
disorder but can't give us the power to change. A friend may
affirm undying devotion and loyalty to us, but guaranteeing it is
something else. A bride and groom can promise each other
never-failing love, but human nature is no match for the
onslaughts of life. These promises often fail for lack of power to
follow through.

We need a word with backing, with power. We not only
need to be told we need to change, but we also need someone to
give us the power to do it. That's where the Bible comes in; it's
the Word of God with power.

The Bible is a transcendent book. It speaks of resources
beyond the natural and the finite. The Bible is not *limited* by its
words, it *begins* with them. Every promise is a key that unlocks
God's vast and limitless resources.

Best of all, the Bible is *for us*. The complete message of

the Bible, as well as its many hundreds of specific promises, are designed to help us and refurbish us in our struggle against the evils of sin and our own wrong desires. The Bible is not an academic, abstract textbook that deals with principles beyond our reach. It is for here and now, today and everyday, perfectly designed to meet each one of our needs.

The Bible Is a Faith-building Book

It not only teaches *about* faith but also *creates* and *builds* faith. There's no doubt that faith is a powerful ingredient in maintaining our emotional and mental health. But faith must have something to feed on! The faith that feeds on speculation or wishful thinking is a fairy-tale faith.

Recently I scoured Psalm 119, the "Word Psalm," to see what it had to say about the power of the Word of God. I was surprised at the results. The psalm lists nineteen beneficial qualities available to the reader and practicer of God's Word. Let's look at them.[1]

The Bible is a *cleansing agent* (vv. 9, 11, 37, 59, 67, 101, 104, 133). The Bible not only shows us the source of cleansing but the Bible itself is a cleansing agent. Jesus said: "You are already clean because of the word I have spoken to you" (John 15:3). Any person who takes in the Bible interestedly, sincerely, and obediently will find that the Bible purifies his or her thoughts, attitudes, and feelings.

The Bible is a *satisfying word* (vv. 14, 24, 35, 47, 72, 77, 92, 103, 111, 127, 129, 162, 174). This satisfaction, this delight is derived not from a mechanical reading of the Bible but from a digesting of the Bible's truths until they enter the deepest parts of our personality and become food and nourishment there.

---

[1] I used the New King James Version for my study; other translations may use slightly different renderings of key words.

155

Practicing Peace

The Bible is a *renewing force* (vv. 25, 40, 107, 154, 156, 159). The use of the words "revive" or "renew" in these verses indicates the endless ability of the Bible to renew our vigor in tackling our problems and growing in our walk with God.

The Bible is a *means of communication between us and God* (v. 26). God often responds to our prayers and needs by a direct message from His Word. I have benefited greatly from "praying the Word," that is, incorporating the words and truths of Scripture into my prayers so that, in a sense, I talk back to God out of His Word. The advantage of this method is that God is able to "talk back" to me from His Word and so give me understanding and guidance. To *pray* the Word as well as *study* the Word is a thoroughly rewarding way to walk in the light as He is in the light.

The Bible *imparts strength* (v. 28). Emotional and mental problems sap and weaken us. Spiritual problems confuse and unnerve us. The tonic needed is the Word, which rebuilds our strength by building confidence through its promises and unbounded optimism.

The Bible *causes the heart to enlarge* (v. 32). A *physically* enlarged heart would be a cause for concern, but a *spiritually* enlarged heart is the most desirable heart to have. When we "run in the way of God's commandments" He enlarges our hearts with the exhilaration of freedom and joy. "When his heart is set free from . . . anxiety, the psalmist will use his liberty for more energetic service" (A. F. Kirkpatrick, *The Book of Psalms*, p. 710). The Bible is a great releaser of new creative energies within us, resulting in joy and radiance.

The Bible *frees us* (v. 45). Jesus equated freedom with truth (John 8:32). To be delivered from poisonous attitudes and feelings, we must know the truth that is able to set us free. To meditate on the Bible is to see ourselves as we really are, with no illusions. The absolute honesty of the Bible makes it our best instrument of healing, even though its truths may be painful to hear and more painful to practice.

The Bible *protects us* (vv. 41–42, 114, 133–134). The Bible is our shield and hiding place. Jesus used this protective power when confronted by Satan on the mountain. Paul reminds us that part of the Christian's armor is the "sword of the Spirit, which is the word of God" (Eph. 6:17). Without the protection of the Bible, we become pitifully vulnerable in a world that, as the poet said, is "no friend to grace."

The Bible *generates hope* (vv. 43, 81, 145–148). The psalmist looks confidently to God's Word as the basis of his trust. When he is cast down, he looks expectantly to the Word as the means of help; he feels he will not be disappointed. The intensity of his cry shows the strength of his confidence in the Word.

The Bible *builds confidence* (vv. 46, 80, 116). When the psalmist talks about not being ashamed, he means not being confused, embarrassed, or overwhelmed. The Bible insulates us against this kind of shame to the point where we can "speak before kings."

The Bible *supplies comfort* (vv. 49–50, 52, 76, 82–83, 143). Various Christian physicians and psychiatrists have told me that they regularly encourage their patients to use Bible reading as the best sleep-producing product available. Psalm 23 is an especially effective calming agent—and it has no side effects!

The Bible *renews and sustains* life (vv. 50, 93, 116). I think it is the *quality* of life the psalmist has in mind in these verses. To be given "life" by the Word means to be brought up to our fullest expression of personal and spiritual power. How do I accomplish this? By a continual absorption of the Word of God.

Practicing Peace

The Bible *imparts wisdom and understanding* (vv. 65–66, 98–104, 130, 144, 169). To be wise in the biblical sense is more than just knowing facts or being liberally educated. Wisdom is closely tied to "understanding," and this in turn is closely related to life (v. 144). Therefore, to be wise is to know how to live successfully (not necessarily to make money or succeed). What value is the accumulation of vast wealth when we nurse the pain of an empty heart or mourn a broken relationship with our spouse, children, friends, or relatives? The pursuit of money is vanity; the pursuit of God is wisdom and understanding. To use the Bible is to become wise.

The Bible *assures us of a purpose for living* (v. 73). To believe that we are "fashioned by God" is to live a meaningful existence. As Viktor Frankl discovered in a concentration camp in World War II, people who found no meaning to their lives lived miserably and died early. To believe that our lives have meaning, powerfully spurs us on to abundant living. The Bible not only assures us that our lives can have meaning, even more it shows us what that meaning is—we are made for an eternal purpose.

The Bible is *a means of guidance* (v. 105). A friend of mine who was negotiating a settlement between a labor union and the company resolved a particularly ugly contract dispute by reading Deuteronomy 15:7–8, 10, in which guidelines for an economic arrangement are laid out. This led to a revised proposal in which both the company and the union were satisfied. If the Bible can guide in financial contracts, then we can trust it to guide our personal matters also.

The Bible *encourages respect* (v. 161). The Bible promotes a healthy respect for God and His Word. In his book *The Knowledge of the Holy,* A. W. Tozer mourned the "loss of religious awe and consciousness of the divine Presence." Tozer claims this "low view of God" is a cause of a "hundred lesser evils" all around us. To be immersed in the Bible is to learn respect for God—a necessary condition for receiving His wisdom, counsel, and blessing.

The Bible *creates personal peace* (v. 165). Paul mentions the "peace in believing," which is a *biblical* peace (Rom. 15:13 KJV). This peace is created by simply trusting that the Word of God is true and reliable. The person who "builds his house on the rock" (that is, hears and obeys the words of Christ) is the person who rests securely when the storm rages.

The Bible *promises deliverance* (vv. 170, 173). When we choose to obey the Word of God, His hand immediately becomes our help and means of rescue. The *Word* of God and the *hand* of God are closely tied together. God's hand is always eager to apply power toward the fulfilling of His Word. If I want God's *hand* to help me, I must use God's *Word* to guide me.

The Bible *restores us* (v. 176). "He restoreth my soul," said David in the beloved Twenty-third Psalm. How does God restore our souls? How does He bring refreshment and new vitality to us? By His Word. Even though we may have strayed like a lost sheep, the Shepherd will search for us and bring us back as we remember His commandments and obey them. Together with prayer, meditating on the Bible is one of the chief ways God brings us back to the rest and contentment of the fold.

As I review these many benefits, I am struck by the fact that it is the Bible itself that is the agent in all of them. This confirms that the Bible is no ordinary book. It is a divine instrument, alive with the presence of God and powerful because it speaks to our hearts and consciences and introduces us to the only Person who can fully satisfy our needs.

In fact, the Bible was given for *people*. God doesn't speak to sticks and stones but to human beings. And as human beings, we can respond to God's words in one of two ways: we can reject them, or we can accept them. Which will it be for us?

The Bible Is a Healing Book

The Bible's methods of healing are as varied as the needs of the human heart. Recently, I came across this letter from a young Christian. She had been fighting a particularly grim battle with feelings of resentment and bitterness.

Jean writes, "I want you to know that God has been working on my attitudes of forgiveness and love lately. I'd like to share with you some things I wrote in my diary recently":

I feel as if I've undergone a real spiritual growing spurt. (God has brought to my attention a serious attitude and showed me some specific direction in correcting it.)

Another thing God brought to my attention lately is my inability to forgive those who have hurt me. I would rehearse their deeds in my mind and talk about them to my husband or anyone who would listen. Then I read this verse: "Do not drag me away with the wicked, with those who do evil, who speak cordially with their neighbors but harbor malice in their hearts" (Ps. 28:3).

Either I was going to ignore these people, or else I was ready to carry out some sort of revenge. Of course I admitted, "I know it's wrong to carry this out, but this is the way I feel." I forgot that God's words about motives and thoughts of the heart are the same as His words about the actions themselves.

Jesus told Peter to forgive a brother who sins against him 490 times. Mind you, this is just for one person! Thinking of the people who have hurt me, not one has overdrawn that account. I doubt they ever will.

The Healing Power of Meditation

I used to say, "I can forgive but I can't forget." I now believe I was wrong. One must forget to truly forgive. Would I want God to remind me or list all He has forgiven me? I don't think I could stand that. Help me to remember, Lord, that each person I know has an account with me. Help me to be as generous in my forgiveness as You have been in Your forgiveness.

Jean's letter went on to explain, "I'm taking action to mend all broken relationships. I've asked God to direct His searchlight on my motives and bring them in line with His purpose. I've slain a bad memory. I put it to death!"

Jean's diary reveals that an honest interfacing with the Word of God, plus a desire to obey God, results in the healing of a poisonous attitude that otherwise would destroy every attempt to walk victoriously in Christ.

Most of us believe that the Bible offers *indirect* benefit in cases of mental and emotional distress. That is, the Bible doesn't cure us, but it makes our problems more bearable.

However, I think evidence indicates that the Bible heals *directly* as well as indirectly. Lately I have been in contact with a young Christian whose wife surprised him one day with the words, "I don't want to be married to you anymore." This statement was followed with something more shocking.

That was the final straw for David. Harassed by personal and other problems, he felt the world was closing in on him. Slowly, he began to sink into the quicksand of discouragement and depression. He began to lose his grasp on his direction in life and its meaning.

Then David did an unusual thing. He did *not* seek out a therapist. He did *not* seek the help of a psychiatrist. He did *not* resort to medicinal help of any kind. He simply went to God in prayer and began a thorough, in-depth reading of the Bible.

First, he scanned the whole Bible and discovered in the

Old and New Testaments an underlying unity that convinced him that this was no run-of-the-mill book. He discovered a divine revelation carefully conveyed by God, using about forty different people to write it. These insights sent his confidence in the Bible soaring. Confidence—that was the beginning.

Next, David studied the life of Job, a sufferer like himself. He noticed that Job underwent incredible sufferings, yet he never denounced God or lost his faith in Him. Lesson number two: don't turn your back on God just because He's allowing you to go through misery and anguish.

Third, David pondered the principles of the Book of James. In the first chapter he learned that wisdom comes from God, that trial and testing (if we endure them patiently) bring us to maturity in wisdom. Wisdom! David thought, how wonderful to be wise in God's eyes!

Putting all three of these things together—David's faith and confidence in the Bible, his faith in God despite his trials, and the reward of being endowed with wisdom as result of his trials—David was able *in two months' time* to emerge from depression and reach stability again.

This is one of the most unusual cases I have run across in my ministry. First, I am impressed by the *speed* of his recovery, and second, I am struck by the directness with which the Bible itself relieved his symptoms. This healing was unusual enough that I have to remind myself (and others) that God doesn't always work that swiftly and directly. And often God uses therapists and medicine as well as His Word.

Yet, there's no doubt that the Bible is a potent weapon against depression. David Seamands sees forty-eight of the one hundred fifty psalms as special medicine for depressed people. He urges his discouraged and depressed counselees to read the psalms aloud, thus affording them a vent for their feelings of alienation and despair, much as the psalmist himself must have done. The psalms Seamands suggests are: 6, 13, 18, 23, 25, 27, 31, 32, 34, 37, 38, 39, 40, 42, 43, 46, 51, 55, 57, 62, 63, 69, 71, 73, 77, 84, 86, 90, 91, 94, 95, 103, 104, 107, 110, 116, 118, 121, 123, 124, 130, 138, 139, 141, 142, 143, 146, 147 (*Healing for Damaged Emotions*, p. 129).

The Bible Must Be an Applied Book

Let me mention first the idea of application or *assimilation*. The problem in much of our Bible reading is that we do it as a habit or custom, which is fine, but it doesn't go far enough. The Bible is intended to become part of us in the *total* sense, body, mind, and spirit.

That's why the Bible describes itself as food to be eaten. When Job refers to the value of the digested Word of God, he says, "I have treasured the words of his mouth more than my daily bread" (Job 23:12). Job's daily bread nourished his body; God's words nourished his total spiritual self.

Jeremiah says, "When your words came, I ate them; they were my joy and my heart's delight" (Jer. 15:16).

God said to Ezekiel, "Son of man, eat this scroll I am giving you and fill your stomach with it" (Ezek. 3:3). So Ezekiel ate it, and it tasted sweet as honey in his mouth.

It's quite evident that when these Bible verses speak of "eating" the Word of God, they mean the complete assimilation. Jesus made the same point when He said: "I am the living bread that came down from heaven. If anyone eats of this bread, he will live forever" (John 6:51). "Eating Jesus" means taking Him completely into our lives. No part of our self can be excluded from His presence and Lordship.

This is what Bible meditation is. "Meditation is sufficient," says Dietrich Bonhoeffer, "if the Word . . . penetrates and dwells within us." He uses words like "ponder," "meditation," "penetration," and "indwelling" to explain the assimilation process of the applied Word.

The Book of Common Prayer says that we must "read, mark, learn, and inwardly digest" the Bible in order to extract the fullest value from it. All this involves pondering the Bible and meditating on it.

Sharing with others what we have learned is another way to "inwardly digest" the Word. Sharing is like writing. It's a sort of oral recap by which we retain what God has revealed to us as we explain it to others.

What about the problem of a *broken connection?* Very often I've heard the complaint (and experienced it myself): "I've tried, but I just don't get anything out of the Bible. I get so discouraged that I give up. Then I feel guilty!" Let me make a few suggestions here.

In order for Bible reading to be meaningful, we must have the right motivation. By motivation I mean the conviction that the Bible has the answer I need. Just as my faith in my doctor's skill encourages me to take the medicine he has prescribed, so my confidence in the Bible motivates me to digest it because I believe that I'll be helped.

Before our meditating will take on meaning, we must make the right decision about our feelings. Very often we let our feelings talk us out of the benefits of the Bible. When our feelings are negative, they can be a stumbling block. Our feelings sometimes say to us: "I'm afraid" or "I don't think it will work" or "Nothing good ever happens to me" or "I wonder if it's all worthwhile" or "I've tried that before" or "Why doesn't God do something?" or "Why does it have to happen to me?"

The real problem here is not the negative feelings themselves but the grip they have on us. The feelings are in charge; they're on top. Everything in our lives must submit to these feelings, and therein lies the danger.

The Healing Power of Meditation

Pitted against these feelings, and standing opposite them, is the Word of God. The issue, therefore, really boils down to this: do I believe my feelings or do I believe His Word?

Here's where we must firmly decide whether the Bible is to become our necessary, soul-feeding storehouse or whether it will be left on the shelf to gather dust. We must shake ourselves free of these negative, deathly feelings and let the Word of God pour its healing strength into our hearts.

In order for the Bible to mean something to us, we must digest the Bible spiritually and personally. By *spiritually* I mean under the tutorship of the same Holy Spirit who wrote it in the first place. Unless we allow Him to apply the Bible's healing truths to us, it will remain just a book of words and sentences. By *personally* I mean to realize that God had *me* in mind when he penned the Word. Just as David could personalize his relationship to God and say, "The Lord is *my* shepherd, *I* shall not want," so I must look for God's personal message to me when I ponder the pages of His Word.

Jane Hollingsworth Haile, a successful Bible teacher, says: "The most important point in any Bible study is this. Look for the message that God has in it for you . . . what bearing does it have on *my* life right now? Obey it implicitly and share it immediately!"

With this approach to the Bible, it won't be long before we'll join King David in saying: "How sweet are your words to my taste, sweeter than honey to my mouth!" (Ps. 119:103 NKJV).

Selah! Think of that.

9

THE HEALING POWER OF
SERVING

As a high school student, I was fascinated with Coleridge's "Rime of the Ancient Mariner," which begins with the gripping words:

> It is an ancient Mariner
> And he stoppeth one of three.
> 'By the long grey beard and glittering eye,
> Now wherefore stopp'st thou me?'

The Mariner detained the unwilling listener with a tale of a south sea voyage on which he had shot an albatross, a large sea bird regarded by early sailors as the bringer of good fortune. As a punishment for his "crime," the Mariner had been made to wear the heavy bird around his neck.

One day, weary with his heavy burden, the Mariner saw a school of sprightly, multicolored fish disporting just beneath the surface of the sea. He was so moved by this unusual sight of brilliant, glittering fish that he raised his heart to heaven and "a spring of love gushed from my heart and I blessed them unaware." Then a curious thing happened: "The Albatross fell off and sank like lead into the sea."

The story, of course, is an allegory. It is also a powerful message: to reach out to others (in this case by prayer) is to relieve ourselves of our own burdens.

What Coleridge said in rhyme is what the Bible says in principle. To help others is to help myself. To share in the healing of others is to bring healing to myself. King Solomon summarized it neatly in his remark about sharing: "A generous man will prosper; he who refreshes others will himself be refreshed" (Prov. 11:25).

THE PSYCHOLOGY OF SERVING

Medical researcher Hans Selye, a specialist on human stress, has emphasized that work is one of the best methods of dealing with stress. The kind of work Selye has in mind is not slavery, which increases stress, but the work that is as enjoyable as play. The need to work, says Selye, is biological. Just as our body becomes flabby if not used, so the brain degenerates into confusion and decay unless we consistently use it in satisfying work.

But there is something more to it than just keeping our brain healthy. Work is not only a biological requirement, it is therapeutic. Selye quotes the Canadian physician, William Osler:

The Healing Power of Serving

Though little, the master word looms large in meaning. It is the "open sesame" to every portal, the great equalizer, the philosopher's stone which transmutes all base metal of humanity into gold. The stupid it will make bright, the bright brilliant, and the brilliant steady. To youth, it brings hope, to the middle-aged confidence, to the aged repose. It is directly responsible for all advances in medicine during the past twenty-five years. Not only has it been the touchstone of progress, but it is the measure of success in everyday life. And the master word is *work* (*Stress Without Distress*, p. 84).

This principle of activity as therapy is well known in modern psychological practice. The old custom of isolating mental patients is now out of favor (except for the most violent patient). The current thinking is directed at getting the patients back into homes, into familiar neighborhoods, and even into productive employment. Meaningful work has played a large part in this new trend toward "healing by doing." In the mental hospitals I've visited recently, I've noticed game rooms, handcraft rooms, and project rooms—a noticeable change from the "caretaking only" treatment I saw earlier in my ministry. Gentle but firm persuasion is used to make the patients express themselves by doing something worthwhile. The energy released, the change of focus from self to others, the shifting of attention to an external, interesting object, all these tend to release tensions and eliminate confusions in the suffering person's mind. Externally directed effort encourages healing.

Let's go a step further. Psychologists have discovered only in the past generation that self-expression is not enough in and of itself. The encouragement to express yourself, prominent in World War II as a therapy for tension, backfired because too often self-expression became "self-explosion," as one New York clergyman expressed it. Too often self-expression became an

169

eruption of selfish desires or frustrations that resulted in drunkenness, sex orgies, or emotional jags induced by drugs.

Self-expression, to be therapeutic, must be a genuine effort to help others. This kind of self-expression is rooted in the desire to serve others and to do it not for the sake of self but for the sake of others. That's what psychologist Gordon Allport means when he says that "self-expression requires the capacity to lose oneself in the pursuit of objectives not primarily referred to the self." True self-expression, in other words, is "other-centered."

This kind of self-expression is thoroughly biblical. It is also rooted in the word *caring*, which is the English equivalent of the Greek word *agape*, which also means "love." The person who cares for others is like the Good Samaritan who helped an unfortunate victim who had been left robbed and wounded on the road (Luke 10:33–35). The Samaritan asked for no reward, sought no advantage; he helped a stranger in distress simply out of the concern of his heart.

I'm sure the Good Samaritan felt twinges of joy at being able to help an unfortunate fellow human being. But there is more than just feeling joy in serving others, there is positive therapeutic benefit.

Edith Schaeffer, in her book *Affliction*, tells of the immature, self-centered young wife who admitted her strong distaste for her husband: "I can't stand him. I can't even stand the sight of him. It makes me feel like vomiting to be in the same room with him." On and on the tirade went as the wife repeatedly used words like "I," "me," "mine," "my right," "my fulfillment," "my life," "my happiness." Not only was her self-centeredness showing, it was putting on a Broadway extravaganza!

Mrs. Schaeffer directed the woman's thoughts into a different channel, one of *positive* self-expression. It was ministry without an awareness of self. It was the illustration of the kernel of wheat falling into the earth and dying to itself in order that others might live.

"Plan a picnic," she advised. But what a picnic! The wife was to fill the basket with the sandwiches, fruit, cookies, and beverages that her husband liked best. She was to encourage him to take the day off to hike together up into the mountains and find a desirable spot. There, after enjoying the nourishing lunch, she was to read to him from a book he would enjoy. Then conversation, not about her gripes and grumbles, but about his interests. The woman was challenged to take this assignment in a deliberate effort to forget herself in the simple pleasure of serving her husband.

Mrs. Schaeffer reports, "She did it. Joy of joys, she did it." And the woman's response was, "I was amazed. It was such an amazing experience. I never thought it could be like that. It was actually a fantastic day." That was the beginning of a deep change in that young wife's life, so deep that when she mangled her hand in a hospital ironer some months later, her only concern was for her husband who had been saddened and worried by the accident. The young wife then asked Mrs. Schaeffer to talk to him because "he really needs help." Deeply touched, Mrs. Schaeffer could only weep when she heard those words of caring from an erstwhile bundle of self-centeredness (p. 166).

The young wife had learned the secret of self-help through caring and serving. Writer Arthur Gordon says, "The more things you care about, the more intensely you care, the more alive you become" (*Reader's Digest*, October 1963, p. 81). This young woman had become truly alive the moment she made her husband's well-being her own. Even more, she found the cure for the destructive self-centeredness that had been eating her life away.

Medical researchers have discovered in the last few years

that there is a direct correlation between the health of our hearts and the well-being of our relationships to others. Where relationships deteriorate, as in the case of death, divorce, or alienation, our hearts can become affected. Dying of a broken heart is no longer considered a quaint expression. It is a sad, continuing fact.

On the other hand, healthy relationships that provide comfort and satisfaction not only sustain an already healthy heart but also strengthen and tone hearts that may have begun to deteriorate. In his book *The Broken Heart*, James. J. Lynch of the University of Maryland has convincingly shown that the human heart is directly affected by the emotional, relational states of the individual. He says, "Human companionship does affect our hearts, and there is reflected in our hearts a biological basis for our need for loving, human relationships."

I have heard many people say, "When my time to die comes, all I want is for some friend or loved one to hold my hand." The companionship of others is recognized as one of the best preparations that earth can provide, far better than medicine or life supports. Best of all, of course, is the presence of the Shepherd, the Lord Jesus, who enables us to say, "Though I walk through the valley of the shadow of death, I will fear no evil: for thou art with me" (Ps. 23:4 KJV).

In this day of family fragmentation, reaching out has become a necessity, not a luxury. Some doctors have found that peptic ulcers are not the result of overwork but underlove. Some types of cancer have been linked to feelings of hopelessness and despair.

The result of all this recent research about the relationship between emotions and health has led to a sharp increase in the need for counseling therapists. Every week or so, it seems, I receive a notice that a new counselor has opened an office in our area. It's understandable!

The Healing Power of Serving

And yet we Christians believe that healing resources are available in the gospel and in the church. We believe that faith in God is the greatest ingredient in emotional health, and the second ingredient in emotional health is the resources of the community of believers.

Paul said to Timothy, "For God did not give us a spirit of timidity, but a spirit of power, of love and of self-discipline" [literally, "sanity"] (2 Tim. 1:7). In accepting Jesus Christ as Savior, we enter a relationship that taps His power, love, and saneness. Sometimes, it is a struggle indeed to appropriate all God has for us, but the resources are there.

God's power can be applied to us directly or indirectly through the body-life principles that operate within the church. Bearing each others' burdens, loving one another, encouraging one another, praying for each other, helping the weak and the afflicted—all of these are practices that enrich us both spiritually and emotionally. "The Church," says Gloria Gaither, "should be the loving fellowship where we can come with our frayed edges, our bruised elbows, our failures and our needs—and be knitted back together, bandaged up, prayed for and loved back to wholeness. Then we can go out, healed and whole and attractive."

SERVING HEALS

Following biblical principles of behavior keeps us emotionally stable. If we suffer emotionally, we can return to these principles to find healing and restoration. God's relationship to us is a *healing* relationship, designed to give us mental and emotional balance as well as robust spiritual health.

The prophet Isaiah understood this dynamic. Isaiah 58 describes how the prophet urged the Israelites to return to God's principles of behavior. He reminded the Israelites that if they would inwardly and outwardly conform to God's will, He would heal their brokenness.

> If you spend yourselves in behalf of the hungry and satisfy the needs of the oppressed, then your light will rise in the darkness, and your night will become like the noonday.
>
> The LORD will guide you always; he will satisfy your needs in a sun-scorched land and will strengthen your frame. You will be like a well-watered garden, like a spring whose waters never fail.
>
> Your people will rebuild the ancient ruins and will raise up the age-old foundations; you will be called Repairer of Broken Walls, Restorer of Streets with Dwellings (Isa. 58:10–12).

Notice that this passage begins with a condition and ends with its consequences. "If you spend yourselves in behalf of the hungry and satisfy the needs of the oppressed." Other translations of this condition are:

> "If you minister to the hungry and satisfy the soul that is bowed down" (Keil and Delitzsch, *Commentary on Isaiah*).
>
> If you extend your soul to the hungry (NKJV).
>
> If you pour yourself out for the hungry (RSV).
>
> If thou draw out thy soul to the hungry (KJV).

The key word in this passage is the Hebrew word *paw-uk*, whose basic meaning is "to furnish or to provide." The thing provided is *oneself*. Whatever the means, whether love or food or money or time, this gift originates from deep within the soul.

George Adam Smith understands this to mean deep Christian commitment: "Tear out what is dear to thee in order to fill his need." The word *paw-uk*, says Dr. Smith, is the "strongest Old Testament expression for self-denial" (*The Book of Isaiah,* p. 419). He sees this self-denial as an example of the self-sacrificing love later described by Paul in his "Love Chapter" (1 Cor. 13).

We are to share ourselves with others as the widow shared her last bit of bread with Elijah, as Mary shared her flask of ointment, as the Good Samaritan shared his oil, wine, and money with a victim of a highway robbery. If we share ourselves this way, the rewards will be great, not only for the ones whom we benefit but also for us.

If we share ourselves with others, we will be given light. "Your light will rise in the darkness, and your night will become like the noonday." Note that this light is in contrast to our *darkness.* If we walk in the darkness of confusion, sharing with others will help diffuse the darkness and bring understanding. If we feel the darkness of depression, living for others will help banish that painful darkness. If we are gripped with the darkness of resentment, offering ourselves in loving ministry to others will directly affect that bitter darkness and dissolve it away. In poetic language Isaiah tells us that the best therapy for unhappy, confused, meaningless life is to live it for others.

If we share ourselves with others, we will be guided. "The LORD will guide you always; he will satisfy your needs in a sun-scorched land and will strengthen your frame [your bones]."

The Lord's guidance here is purposeful. He guides us from something to something. When we are drying up in a scorching land, He will guide us to springs of water (v. 11). When we are fainting with weariness because of life's piled-up troubles, He will lead us to strength and vitality. The simple principle here is that as we pour ourselves out for needy people, God will replenish our ability and strength to share so that we will continue to *increase* in the ability to share. The supply will not run out; the well will not go dry; the bush will continue to burn without being consumed.

Practicing Peace

The self-centered life is a wasted life. It lives for the moment, spinning around and around in the inane desire to please itself. The self-centered person is bound to become emotionally crippled because God never made us that way. We became that way because of sin. I've heard many emotional cripples say, "I feel lost and drifting. I have no fixed purpose." On the other hand, people who are dedicated to Jesus Christ and to the needs of others are focused people. The threads of their lives no longer unravel but are knit as one whole.

If we share ourselves with others, we will become fruitful. "You will be like a well-watered garden, like a spring whose waters never fail." Spiritual and emotional help comes from offering our love and help to others. This kind of a Christian, says George Adam Smith, "grows rich and life [becomes] joyful, by the acts of service with the warm heart of love."

The biblical example of this fruitfulness is Joseph. His father, Jacob, described him as "a fruitful vine, a fruitful vine near a spring, whose branches climb over a wall" (Gen. 49:22). This is a remarkable tribute to a son. Jacob likened his son to a fruitful vine because Joseph was a self-sacrificing, generous person. Despite his family's hatred of him, Joseph served his brothers. As a young boy he served them in the fields. Years later, when he was a leader in Egypt, Joseph reconciled himself to his famine-stricken brothers and provided food for them. Later he made a home for them in Egypt. Joseph poured himself out for others.

We might be tempted to say, "Joseph was a special case!" But Isaiah's promise is addressed to everyone. Becoming a sharing person requires compassion, not gifts. Jesus did not make sharing an option for the elite but a command for every believer.

If we share ourselves with others, we will become Repairers of Broken Walls. This means we become constructive and

176

useful. I once saw a sign on a fixit shop, "We mend everything but broken hearts." But God can mend even those. How does He do it? God's method is always people.

Emotionally disturbed people are often *imprisoned* people. They are like Samson, blinded and grinding corn for the Philistines. Their chains may not be iron, but they are more powerful and devastating: fears, jealousies, hatreds, resentments, insecurities, and the rest. God wants us to deliver the emotionally bound person. This is what Jesus, the great Fettercutter, came to do.

> The LORD has anointed me to preach good news to the poor. He has sent me to bind up the brokenhearted, to proclaim freedom for the captives and release from darkness for the prisoners, to proclaim the year of the Lord's favor and the day of vengeance of our God, to comfort all who mourn, and provide for those who grieve in Zion—to bestow on them a crown of beauty instead of ashes, the oil of gladness instead of mourning, and a garment of praise instead of a spirit of despair (Isa. 61:1– 3).

When Jesus lives out His life in us, we can expect to be changed into "heart binders," "freedom preachers," "prisoner releasers," and "grief comforters" as Jesus was. The basis of Christ's ministry is compassion, and compassion pulls down the destroying walls and builds the walls of peace and safety.

Jesus is the Mender of Broken Hearts; His restorative powers are far beyond the capability of any psychiatrist or therapist. He invites us to join Him in that ministry of repairing and restoring.

PRACTICAL WAYS TO SERVE

When Admiral Richard E. Byrd experimented with living alone during his seven months stay in isolation at the South Pole, he began to suffer various kinds of strange emotional illnesses. He came to the conclusion that human beings were not destined to live alone. In his book *Alone*, he says, "I don't think that a man can do without sounds and smells and voices and touch, anymore than he can do without phosphorus and calcium."

What Byrd discovered by experiment God had already revealed through His Word. "It is not good for the man to be alone" (Gen. 2:18). If perfect Adam needed companionship, what about *imperfect* Adam? The tragedy of our imperfectness is that it breeds a variety of emotional as well as spiritual problems. Sin separates us from God; emotional problems separate us from each other. For example, British psychologist John Bowlby says that "impairment of attraction" is one of the causes of emotional and psychological difficulties today. By "impairment of attraction" Bowlby means the hatred, bitterness, and rejection that often infest the family unit. No doubt he is right. But we need to add that impairment of attraction has been an integral part of the human race since Adam's fall.

This broken relationship with others is often a cause of heart problems. In his book *The Broken Heart*, James Lynch maintains that isolation, loneliness, and lack of companionship are just as devastating on the human heart as smoking, stress, and lack of exercise.

It is a known fact also that infants deprived of love and cuddling do not thrive. In fact, many die. Despite adequate diets and professional care, these little ones need something more—love and comfort expressed in cuddling and caressing.

These facts argue for the ministry of caring and sharing. "Love one another" is a command designed not only to keep us spiritually alive but also to keep us emotionally alive.

In what ways can we reach out in ministry? How can we share ourselves with others?

We can serve by listening. German theologian Dietrich

The Healing Power of Serving

Bonhoeffer said listening to others was the number one ministry to others. In *Life Together*, he says, "The first service that one owes to others in the fellowship consists in listening to them." Bonhoeffer calls listening "soul therapy." He laments that secular therapists have captured a healing art that ought to be practiced by every Christian.

The therapeutic value of listening to others is reinforced by Professor Earle Koile of the University of Texas in his book *Listening as a Way of Becoming*. "Clues for a happier, more effective life may be found when we can listen sensitively and openly to others and they to us. Moreover, in such interchanges, we may find healthy outlets for our anger and frustration, richer ways to experience love and joy and, in short, find new dimensions of our humanness."

Listening, however, is not a passive, easy way to victory. To listen therapeutically we must not listen judgmentally or disdainfully but *empathetically*. This means to put ourselves in the shoes of the speaker and identify with him or her. We must mentally think out the other person's experience. Only by this kind of "losing ourselves" for the sake of others can we gain a richer life for ourselves.

But the benefits are great. "The language of sharing and listening, experienced in personal terms," says Dr. Koile, "offers relief from boredom, loneliness, and anxiety."

Let's add a new beatitude: "Blessed are the listeners, for they shall enrich their own hearts also."

We can serve by bearing. The apostle Paul commands us: "Carry each other's burdens, and in this way you will fulfill the law of Christ" (Gal. 6:2). The law of Christ was the way Christ Himself acted who "took up our infirmities and carried our sorrows" (Isa. 53:4).

Bearing means something different for every person. For some, it means paying another person's rent. For others, it means caring for someone's children. For others, it means lending a listening ear.

One way to bear the burden of another is simply to *understand*. Henri Nouwen says in *Out of Solitude*, "When we honestly ask ourselves which person in our lives mean most to us, we often find that it is those who, instead of giving much advice, solutions, or cures, have chosen rather to share our pain and touch our wounds with a gentle and tender hand."

From the days of Job to the present, one of the greatest needs of the human sufferer is to be understood. Most people can bear pain and anguish if they can be supported by the simple yet marvelous practice of just being understood.

We don't have to have identical experiences in order to understand. Jesus doesn't know what it is to sin, but He is the great Comforter of sinners. We comfort people by simply indicating by word or gesture that we feel the pain they feel. We read that Jesus "became us" (Heb. 7:26 KJV), that is, He becomes so identified with us that the pain we feel is the pain He feels; thus He is able to meet our need (v. 26 NIV).

In order to understand others, especially *suffering* others, we must make a determined act of the will. But in that determination and self-forgetfulness of entering into the lives and experiences of others, we discover ourselves being made whole.

We can serve by talking. Nobody needs to be told that talking is therapy. Emotionally afflicted people tend to isolate themselves from others, usually as a defense mechanism. Hurt people don't want to keep on getting hurt, so they avoid the people and circumstances that are likely to produce further hurt. However, this avoidance only compounds the problem. "Go out, see people, do things!" one person advised a depressed friend.

"But I don't *feel* like it," was the response.

"Exactly," was the reply, "and the less you go, the more you won't feel like it."

The Healing Power of Serving

The friend took the advice, forced himself to go out and meet people and talk to them, all the while wishing he were back in his room nursing his grief alone. But in time the therapy worked. The springs of emotional health and confidence began to seep, then flow, then bubble within his spirit.

A good way to begin conversation with another ailing person is to ask yourself, "What would I want people to say to me in the same situation?" A general rule for a topic of conversation should be, make it *affirmative*. Negative, critical comments are like a galloping virus that spreads and worsens as it goes. Affirmative, supportive comments (no platitudes, though) are a tonic to the suffering spirit.

A pastor's wife was suffering from a bout of depression. She complained to her husband, "I can't pray. I can't read the Bible. I don't feel I'm much of a Christian."

The answer was, "Don't worry about praying or reading. God knows your heart. He also knows your nervous system. Just rest in Him and trust Him to carry you through." After she recovered from her affliction, she told her husband that his supportive words had meant more to her than any other kind of therapy. The words were affirmative and healing.

Let's not pontificate. "You shouldn't feel that way!" is poor advice for a sufferer; it simply expands the guilt. Another poor conversation starter is, "I know how you feel." No, we don't. No human being knows exactly what another human being is going through. We are too different from each other. No facet of a diamond catches the sunlight in exactly the same way as any other facet. So with us. It's much better to say, "I don't know what you're going through, but I can feel your pain and I sympathize." Your conversation will be doubly effective if the person you talk to is convinced of your sincerity and unselfishness.

The power of healing conversation is mighty indeed. Isaiah

described it this way: "How beautiful on the mountains are the feet of those who bring good news, who proclaim peace, who bring good tidings, who proclaim salvation [deliverance], who say to Zion, 'Your God reigns!' " (Isa. 52:7).

How often we throw those verses at some deserving missionaries, feeling the words apply to them and them only. But read those verses again. Think of a suffering soul reaching out to another sufferer with helpful words. Consider the power of such words as "good news," "peace," "good tidings," "deliverance," and the livingness of God! Every word is positive, assertive, and uplifting. So must our words be positive.

We can serve by helping. The Bible calls this the gift of "helps" (1 Cor. 12:28 KJV). A help can be anything from giving another person a small gift to baby-sitting for a young couple so they can attend a special meeting at the church. The value of such help is not in what is done or contributed but in the effect it has on both the givers and the receivers. The receivers are benefited because their lives are made easier. The givers are benefited because they have toned up their feelings of self-worth.

A newly born-again Christian went to see the owner (also a Christian) of a drug store about a desire she had. "I'd like to do something for the pastor," she said, "just to show him my appreciation. But I don't know how to go about it."

"How about buying him a small office radio?" suggested the druggist. "I know he doesn't have one."

"Oh, I don't know," she replied. "Would he be offended? Would I be presumptuous?"

"Do it!" the druggist insisted.

She bought the radio, presented it to the pastor, then returned a little while later to the store and beamed, "I feel wonderful!"

This woman did something for her pastor, yes, but I think she did far more for herself. What her gift said to her was that she was a kind, caring, generous, and considerate person. Without even knowing it, she was giving herself a hefty emotional boost, and she lived on the strength of it for many days.

The principle that to help others is to enrich ourselves is borne out by a study made by the Connecticut Mutual Insurance Company in 1981. The company polled a number of Americans to ask about their beliefs. The study revealed that seventy-five percent of those polled admitted to being Christians, but only one-third admitted to being *dedicated* Christians. The dedicated ones were those who confessed to being born again, who attended church regularly, and who shared their lives with others in such things as encouraging others, sharing the Word of God with others, and in doing community service. The level of satisfaction with their lives was sharply higher among the dedicated Christians than among the nominal ones. This poll is simply a modern illustration of the timeless truth of God's Word: "Cast your bread upon the waters, for after many days you will find it again" (Eccl. 11:1).

Jesus stated this principle in that well-known statement in Luke: "Give, and it will be given to you. A good measure, pressed down, shaken together and running over, will be poured into your lap. For with the measure you use, it will be measured to you" (Luke 6:38). Simply stated, to share with others is to receive; to talk to others is to benefit myself; to extend a helping hand to others is to receive the same help in return—only multiplied.

The gospel of Jesus Christ is not only a theological gospel, it is a psychological gospel. The person who obeys the teaching of the Word and lives for the betterment of other people achieves a double purpose: the uplifting of society and the uplifting of his or her own heart. It is by losing our lives we find them and by dying for His sake we live.

CONCLUSION

As you have discovered in reading this book, the gospel of Jesus Christ heals us. Jesus Christ came to make us whole, and this wholeness is one, just as we human beings are one person. The forgiveness of sins that Jesus died for on the cross results in more than just removing the *charge* of sin against us; it also erases all the damage that sin has done to our minds, emotions, and will.

So we shouldn't be surprised when we discover that by doing what God wants us to do—praise Him, pray to Him, meditate on Him in the Word, confess our sins, love one another, serve others, trust Him, forgive others, and put our hope in Him—we find healing for the hurting parts of our souls and spirits. Says J. A. Hadfield, an English psychiatrist of a generation ago, "I am convinced that the Christian religion is one of the most valuable and potent influences for producing that harmony and peace of mind and that confidence of soul which is needed to bring health and power to a large proportion of nervous patients." This was written in a day when psychiatry was suspicious of Christianity and often accused it of making our emotional ills *worse.* Hadfield maintained the opposite: Christianity heals those ills.

We need healing because we are born disintegrated. We are at odds with God, ourselves, and others. Faith in Jesus Christ brings a correction of those relationships. "We have peace with God" says Paul (Rom. 5:1). We also have peace with ourselves, the peace "of God" (Phil. 4:7). To complete the triumvirate, we can have peace with each other, "live at peace with everyone" (Rom. 12:18). The gospel has more than a vertical effect; it also has a horizontal effect.

However, here's an important matter to think about. Total healing is not automatic at conversion. Our sins are forgiven, indeed, but the effect of that sin in our bodies, minds, and emotions will need constant, faithful treatment. Some people make great strides in emotional healing as well as spiritual, while others are laggards and suffer. Some of the great saints in church history suffered agonizingly with emotional ills like depression, discouragement, loneliness, and jealousy. However, consider what those saints would have been like *without* the healing power of the gospel.

In any book of this type there is always the problem of selection of material. Because the field is so vast, I had to be individualistic in my choice of chapter headings. I'm sure someone will wonder why I did not include a chapter on "worship." "Certainly worship has healing power," they will say. I agree. My only problem with worship was knowing how to isolate it from all the other things I've said in this book. After all, if worship, broadly speaking, is "an encounter with God," then worship is present in all of my chapters. If we adopt Francois Fenelon's definition of worship as "a simple movement of the heart toward God," then every Christian practice I've alluded to in this work would constitute worship.

186

Conclusion

Of course I realize that worship can be specific. There can be *solitary* worship, the simple adoration of God by the side of the sea or in the midst of the mountain peaks or under the stars. Whenever this experience occurs there is bound to be an uplift of soul that invigorates the whole person.

Then there is *corporate* worship. This joining of persons and voice with others in adoring God most certainly brings its benefits. Only those who are denied such opportunities because of illness or frailty can fully appreciate how much worship means to their sense of well being.

But there is another kind of worship, the kind I've incorporated into this book, *ordinary* worship. This is the worship of God expressed in helping an unlettered person read the Bible, carrying a basket of groceries to a needy family, encouraging a sick friend by a warm visit. If all of these are done in the name of the Lord, they too constitute worship. This is in keeping with the words of James: "Religion that God our Father accepts as pure and faultless is this: to look after orphans and widows in their distress and to keep oneself from being polluted by the world" (James 1:27). If this is pure religion, then it has benefits for the one who practices it.

I am more convinced than ever that a simple living of the Christian life will go a long way toward making our lives fruitful and happy. In their book *Psychosomatics*, Howard and Martha Lewis relate the experiences of two mothers whose sons were taken seriously ill. Nancy's son developed leukemia, while Arlene's son was diagnosed with a malignant tumor.

Nancy was a Christian. She said, "God is in complete control. He is using our family and this disease to bring His message to the world." As a result of this simple, deep faith in God, Nancy suffered no impairment of health or symptoms of mental and emotional stress.

Arlene, on the other hand, had no such faith in God. Her

187

son's dangerous condition gave her feelings of dread from which she couldn't escape. Functionally, she began to exhibit stress symptoms. Her relationship with her husband deteriorated, and she began to eat and drink heavily.

This simple account points up the difference between having faith and hope in God and trying to make it on your own. Not all Christians, of course, will have strength as Nancy did. Nor do all non-Christians fall apart as Arlene did. Nevertheless it is the testimony of psychiatry, physiology, and medical science, as well as religion, that the person who trusts God and has hope in Him will do better in a trying situation than one who has no such faith or hope at all.

The whole matter can be summed up by Augustine. "For thou hast stirred [us] up that [we] may take pleasure in praising thee; because thou hast created us for thyself, and our heart knows no rest, until it may repose in thee" (*Confessions*, p. 31).

To put it briefly, God is not only necessary for us, He is good for us. God is not only the source of our life, He is our health; God is not only our Savior and Redeemer, He is "the strength of [our] life" (Ps. 27:1 KJV).

BIBLIOGRAPHY

Baker, Don. *Beyond Forgiveness*. Portland, Oregon: Multnomah Press, 1984.

Bonhoeffer, Dietrich. *Life Together*. New York: Harper and Row, 1954.

Brand, Paul, and Philip Yancey. *Fearfully and Wonderfully Made*. Grand Rapids, Michigan: Zondervan Publishing House, 1980.

Burroughs, Jeremiah. *The Rare Jewel of Christian Contentment*. Grand Rapids, Michigan: Sovereign Grace Publishers, 1971.

Frankl, Viktor. *The Doctor and the Soul*. New York: Bantam Books, 1967.

Fromm, Erich. *The Art of Loving*. New York: Harper and Row, 1956.

Gillquist, Peter. *Love Is Now*. Grand Rapids, Michigan: Zondervan Publishing House, 1970.

James, William. *The Will to Believe*. New York: Longmans, Green, 1897.

Johnson, Paul. *The Psychology of Pastoral Care*. Nashville, Tennessee: Abingdon Press, 1953.

Koile, Earle. *Listening as a Way of Becoming*. Waco, Texas: Word Books, 1977.

Liebman, Joshua Loth. *Peace of Mind*. New York: Simon and Schuster, 1946.

Lockyer, Herbert. *All the Prayers of the Bible*. Grand Rapids, Michigan: Zondervan Publishing House, 1959.

Lynch, James J. *The Broken Heart*. New York: Basic Books, 1977.

Practicing Peace

MacArthur, John. *Why Believe in the Bible*. Ventura, California: Regal Books, 1978.

McDowell, Josh. *Evidence That Demands a Verdict*. San Bernardino, California: Here's Life Publishers, 1979.

Nouwen, Henri. *Out of Solitude*. South Bend, Indiana: Ave Maria Press, 1974.

Schaeffer, Edith. *Affliction*. Old Tappan, New Jersey: Fleming H. Revell, 1978.

Seamands, David. *Healing for Damaged Emotions*. Wheaton, Illinois: Victor Books, 1981.

Smedes, Lewis B. *Forgive and Forget*. San Francisco: Harper and Row, 1984.

Taylor, Dr. and Mrs. Howard. *Hudson Taylor's Spiritual Secret*. London: China Inland Mission, 1932.

Thielicke, Helmut. *I Believe*. Philadelphia: Fortress Press, 1968.

Tournier, Paul. *Guilt and Grace*. New York: Harper and Row, 1962.
_____. *The Meaning of Persons*. New York: Harper and Row, 1957.

Tozer, A. W. *The Knowledge of the Holy*. New York: Harper Brothers, 1961.

White, John. *Masks of Melancholy*. Downers Grove, Illinois: InterVarsity Press, 1982.